Contents

Introduction

By David Aikman

During the five days of September 7-11, 1975 more than 430 delegates from 23 countries gathered in Manila for an unusual conference. It was called "Love China '75" and set itself a task that only a few years ago many would have considered too absurd to contemplate: how to give the Chinese people the best opportunity to hear the Gospel of Jesus Christ. Put simply, "Love China '75" was the first full-scale gathering anywhere in the world of evangelicals concerned about the Christian witness in China since the Communist government gained power in 1949.

During the conference, perhaps more aptly termed a seminar by the organizers, the participants heard a variety of speakers address several topics integral with the presentation of the Christian Gospel in China. They heard young Chinese pastors, old Western missionaries, lay people, Protestants, a Catholic, even one spellbinding Welshman who had been converted

during the great Welsh revival of 1904. The later
sessions of Love China '75 permitted participants
to exchange their own views with the speakers. In
between the formal sessions there were countless
informal smaller gatherings of participants and
speakers. At the end of each day there was
always a time of informal prayer together for
China, for the Christians there, for those who
had never known about Christ's promises to the
human race, and for the greater effectiveness of
the speakers and participants, all by now deeply
humbled in their coming together.

One of the surprises of the conference was
the exceptional sense of unity present. No less
than 15 different Christian denominations and
55 different missionary organizations were represented, and all of them were not merely still
loving each other when the conference ended,
but had learned to appreciate each other's work in
ways they had not previously thought possible.
The Lord was present, and all of us there sensed
it.

There was a strong temptation to bring out
a book on Love China '75 very quickly after the
conference ended. Pressures of other work on
the organizers and the editor, however, made
this impossible. Now, in a sense, the delay has
emerged as a blessing. The year 1976 was utterly
cataclysmic for China, and not even the wisest
person at Love China '75 could have predicted
the upheavals which would ravage the country in

the Year of the Dragon. Despite the tragedies of China's natural disasters, from a Christian standpoint, there is much cause for rejoicing. Not only has China's internal situation offered much greater promise than before of potential receptivity to the Gospel, but the whole thrust of Love China '75, the emphasis on bringing the message of Christ to China in both humility and love, has been entirely vindicated by China's own growing awareness of internal fallibility.

The year 1976 started on a somber note. Early in January, as the inhabitants of Peking were bundling themselves against the fierce North China winter, Premier Chou En-lai died. Despite the obvious criticisms that can be made of him as a statesman determined to advance domestically and internationally the cause of Communism, Chou was genuinely loved by most Chinese. Amid an array of grim-faced, and often crude political figures at the highest level of the Chinese government, Chou had a well-deserved reputation for cultivation, modesty, unselfishness, and great personal kindness. I was in Peking the day following his funeral, and I can attest from numerous incidents how widespread the admiration for him was.

But political reputations do not often these days survive the struggles among his successors that follow a great man's departure. Chou's influence was quickly eclipsed by an intense, leftist-inspired campaign to oust from power his

apparent protege and successor, Vice-Premier
Teng Hsiao-p'ing. Teng, a tough negotiator and
brilliant administrator, had already been the
target of ideological wrath in 1966, when he was
removed from high party power during the
Cultural Revolution. In April 1976, however, his
political opponents struck hard again. Shortly
after violent riots had broken out in Peking's
T'ien An Men Square to protest against the removal of commemorative wreaths for Chou En-lai
on the occasion of Ch'ing ming, China's festival in
honor of the deceased, Teng was stripped of all
party and government posts. The move was
resented at most levels in China, not so much
because Teng was universally beloved, as because
he seemed to offer to most Chinese a pragmatic,
common-sense approach to solving China's not
inconsiderable economic and social problems.

Teng's removal from the scene did not calm
China down. Go-slows in factories, pilferage and
petty crime increased in several parts of the
country in the spring and summer of 1976. Then
in July another cataclysm occurred. An earthquake of quite appalling severity rocked China's
Northeast, damaging Tientsin severely and even
rocking Peking. Worst of all, however, was the
complete obliteration of China's major Northern
mining city, T'angshan, whose population was
around 1.2 million. The Chinese government
never revealed to the outside world the extent of
the damage or loss of life, but there is evidence

to suggest that the disaster was possibly the second worst earthquake in the recorded history of the world. In the total area there were more than a million casualties, of whom, according to one source, 655,000 were deaths. The country bravely tried to put the best face on things. As after-shocks rumbled on, most of Peking's Chinese residents lived outside on the streets and sidewalks, camping in makeshift huts and tents.

China's great leader, meanwhile, was clearly slipping fast. Though Mao's death had been repeatedly rumored as imminent for a decade or more, from July on no more foreign visitors were permitted to see him. As much to the Chinese as to the outside world, this was indeed the sign that the Chairman's passing was not far off, awesome as such an event would surely be. On September 9, he went "to see God," as he himself had sometimes graphically put it to his colleagues and to foreigners. There followed a chilling few weeks of complete indecision within China's top leadership. While Mao lay in state for several days, mourned officially by selected Chinese and by many foreigners who were permitted to walk past the bier, no one really seemed to be at China's helm. A particularly odd hesitation was evident over what ought to be done with Mao's body. Would he be cremated, as one Chinese official said had been his wish, or would he be embalmed for future generations, like Lenin in Moscow's Red Square? Everyone held his breath.

A relatively unknown Chinese leader, Hua Kuo-feng, read the memorial address in the T'ien An Men Square to massed ranks of workers, peasants, and military personnel on September 18. Hua had unexpectedly — to outside observers — been named Acting Premier after Chou En-lai died, signalling clearly that Teng Hsiao-p'ing would not succeed to the premiership. Now, in September, Hua seemed to loom larger than ever, the job confirmed officially some months earlier, and his rather jowly physical presence dominating the rostrum from which the September memorial address was delivered. Hua looked as though he might soon be made Chairman of the Communist Party in succession to Mao.

Before everything fell into place there was another cataclysm. As rumors spread around China in early October that the Central Committee of the Communist Party was preparing to elevate Hua officially, an astonishing piece of news was deliberately leaked by Communist officials in Peking to Western correspondents stationed in the Chinese capital. All four of China's top Politburo figures associated with the more radical or "leftist" policies since the Cultural Revolution ten years earlier, had been arrested by members of Hua's personal bodyguard. The most famous of these was none other than Mao's wife Chiang Ch'ing, a sometime

movie actress who had attracted Mao's attention
during the Communist Party's years of struggle
in Yenan during the 1930s. Chiang Ch'ing was
widely disliked in China because of her sharp
and at times personally vindictive tongue. Her
political allies, all Shanghai-based figures, Chang
Ch'un-ch'iao, Wang Hung-wen and Yao Wen-
yuan, had time and again been architects of
strongly ideological campaigns aimed at preserving the egalitarian thrust of the Cultural
Revolution and, supposedly, maintaining China's
revolutionary purity from contact with the cor-
rupting habits of the West and the outside world
in general. The "Gang of Four," as China's
official press swiftly labelled them, were no
friends of Chou En-lai, not to mention Teng
Hsiao-p'ing, whom they had hounded from
power twice, in 1966 and 1976.

Most outside observers deemed Hua's arrest
of the Gang as a victory for China's army com-
manders, generally older men who had little
interest in the minutiae of ideological campaigns
every few months, and for the so-called
"moderates," government and party adherents
of Chou En-lai's gradualist approach both to
domestic policy and international relations.
China's official press, now in the hands of Hua
and his allies, soon dropped the endless tirades
against the already demoted Teng Hsiao-p'ing
and turned their rodomontades upon the "Gang
of Four." Lurid accounts were printed and

broadcast of how decadent and selfish Chiang
Ch'ing had allegedly been, and how the Gang
had been responsible for virtually everything
that had gone wrong in China for several years.
Even the twice-disgraced Teng Hsiao-p'ing in
early 1977 looked as if he would soon be given
an important job again. At the time of this writing, in
late 1978, as Party Vice-Chairman and Deputy Prime
Minister, he even looks as though he is attempting to
edge out Mao's designated successor Hua Kuo-feng.

The details and tone of such recrimina-
tions, to be sure, are even today enough to cause
a glazing over of the eyes of all but the most
eager Chinawatcher or academician. Even the
news at the end of 1976 of serious factional
fighting in numerous parts of China between
supporters of Hua and diehard adherents of
Chiang Ch'ing did not really help the ordinary
layman understand China better. To the Christian primarily concerned with the openness of
China to the Gospel the upheavals of 1976,
though tragic and deserving great sympathy
as well as the political infighting today, might
perhaps be regarded in some respects as not really
germane to that central issue.

Yet this almost cynical view of China in the
throes of yet another domestic upheaval would
be wrong. The fact is that the arrest of the
"Gang of Four" in October 1976 was widely
popular throughout China. Such exuberance in
particular at Chiang Ch'ing's downfall indicates

how intensely resented the heavily ideological policies of the Cultural Revolution had become over the years. The idealism of the Red Guards was, in fact, crushed by Mao's demand in the late 1960s that all educated Chinese youth should not only spend some time in the countryside but in certain instances should spend their whole lives there. The endless political tirades over factory loudspeakers, the constant hectoring by the People's Daily, the tedious and verbose political formulae which had to be learned by heart and studied at weary evening meetings: all these had also taken a toll on the sensibilities of ordinary Chinese. Those who leave China today report a widespread cynicism among Chinese of all ages and a hunger for solid values, for stability, and for basic honesty in social and political relations.

It is these very human needs that the Christian Gospel meets more satisfactorily and totally than any other belief system in the world. The Chinese people do not, in fact, want another set of political beliefs or another ideological creed in addition to what they already have. They want a friend, a Comforter, and a hope that will not fade. It is inconceivable that any Christian who has tasted of the intimacy and balm of the personal lordship of Christ could wish otherwise than to seek to make available to Chinese in China the knowledge of such a Friend. So it is even today, more than ever before, nearly 18 months after Love China '75 came to an end in Manila.

The addresses and discussions in this book speak for themselves. No attempt has been made in the editing to produce uniformity in the sentiment or the manner of expression. Yet it is strangely exciting to observe what a sense of united purpose and urgency does emerge from so many of the chapters included within these covers. I personally believe the hand of the Lord was present throughout all of Love China '75 and that the message is more dramatic, more thrilling, and more immediate now even than it was in 1975. It is still, before anything else, a message to China of love. "Lord Jesus, through us, let the people feel your love," was the motto printed from beginning to end of the Love China '75 program manual. And so it is now that this book, a summation and updating of the Love China '75 addresses, is called Love China Today.

David Aikman, January 1977.

Foreword

Why China?

By Brother Andrew

I want to give you a brief background to this conference. In Europe, we are 25 years ahead of Asia in this revolution, but also, in coming to grips with this particular situation. In Western Europe, there are 20 missions that are coming together that have now reached into the Communist countries. They effectively share information, they pool their resources and they plan strategy. In these years, much has been accomplished, but much more remains to be done. And yet, Russian believers have said that today there are more Bibles in Russia than ever before. In fact today, there are more believers in Russia than ever before. Asia — the revolution here came 25 years later. The revolution here is still being led by the creative minority. It is still developing its philosophy. And yet there is already a greater area behind the Bamboo Curtain than there is in Europe behind the Iron Curtain. There's a greater population, there's a greater threat. Greater need and greater problems. But we have not yet reached a unity among the missions. We have not yet developed a strategy because we do not know of one. The apostle Paul said, "We are not ignorant of his devices", but *we* are ignorant. That is a big problem.

The Bible says here in Ephesians 6 that we do not wrestle against flesh and blood. That is not the only problem. In addition there is a watered-down Christianity that seems to have no answer to the mounting problems of our time, and that spends its time fighting itself instead of fighting the devil. We are here this week to study, to begin to understand more, but also to realize what we are in Christ Jesus. The perfect breeding ground for Communism is man at war, man at war with himself, with society, with racism, with labor conditions, with politics, with corruption, with religious conflicts, with poverty and injustice, and with famine. And you must understand this: that all of these conflicts will be cultivated because every country changes by conflict until it finally ends up in Communism. According to Christian philosophy, the church has undoubtedly the answer to all of those problems, but the individual Christian must first solve these problems for himself before God can use him to be part of their overall solution. This is, in my honest opinion, the only way to counteract and to prevent revolution. You see, social reform will be the direct result of revival and reformation.

There's something wonderful about the Great Commission that Jesus Christ gave us. The Great Commission focuses on the end result. Matt. 28, verse 19 — "Disciples of all nations." Matt. 24, verse 14 — "This Gospel of the Kingdom shall be preached to all nations." And then, Mark 13, verse 10 — it says, "It must first be preached to all nations." Jesus did not focus on the resources, although they too are limitless. "All authority in heaven and on earth have been given to me," He said. Note that Jesus did not focus on specific methods. Jesus simply gave the initiative to the Church, and that initiative is valid until the consummation of time. You want another word for revolution? Initiative. But the moment a man moves out of the crowd to take initiative, he becomes a target. That scares too many people away from doing the will of God. Yet only initiative pays. Some call it faith, active faith. But those who stay in the crowd and who conform to the crowd will certainly never change the world. Jesus set the goal and He lets us choose the methods. He shared His authority and gave us the power of the Holy Spirit. Now nothing moves in this world until it is moved by some force greater than itself. Of course, the things to be moved will not consent to it. They will fight back with fierce accusations, as with the Jews in Thessalonica, where they said,

"These men that have turned the world upside down have come here too." In fact they had not turned the world upside down. That's what the devil had done. The apostles simply came to put it upside up again. And in Thessalonica, they were accused of having contravened the laws of Caesar. Of course, they had to break the laws of Godless governments.

Indeed, if we are fully to obey the laws of God, we will have to break many other laws. In other words, if you want to keep every law, you are going to break the law of God. The apostles also faced this: "They teach there is another King, Jesus." And that is correct. There is another Kingdom, and Matt. 28, verse 18 anticipates the clash between the Kingdom of God and the systems of the world. Peter proclaimed this in Acts 5: 29, "We must obey God rather than man." Peter proclaimed that in Acts 17, verse 7. And in Acts 14, verse 22. Those verses tell us about the cause of this conflict. We have to go through many tribulations into the Kingdom of God. But I have to make one thing very clear tonight. The Kingdom of God is not a reality and it is not understood and not believed and preached as long as we accept the status quo, the status quo of political and nationalistic frontiers. Here are two totally opposed concepts. But God's Word says, "According to your faith, be it unto you." If we say the doors are closed, then they are closed. And if we say the doors are open, then they are open. And then, on the basis of that profession of faith, God will then give us the faith to go because we have honored Him and His Word.

Now, faith means accepting the open doors concept: simply planning and then moving in, realizing that when Jesus sent His disciples into the world He sent them into enemy-occupied territories. When Jesus said, "I have all authority in Heaven and on earth," He made an almost political statement. We must attempt to do for God and for the suffering Church so much that unless the Almighty God intervenes, we're doomed to fail. And that requires a willingness to be made a fool for Christ. And organizations and missions that explicitly state that they only work in countries where this is legal, they are missing the boat in this end time. Soon, it will not be legal anywhere in the world. You say, "Brother Andrew, how do you know that?" Because Jesus said, "The night cometh in which no man can work." That's why today, we rejoice in the ministry of the FEBC here in Manila. It's really a matter of principles what I'm saying now. You see, what they do is just as illegal as what some of our missions do. Only, there is no physical risk involved. But we sure are comrades-in-arms.

If only we could see it — God's world. The strong point in the Kingdom of God's message and approach is that we have an unshakeable truth. I am so glad about this book our Bible. No philosophy and no politician and certainly not Communism can claim its claims. They have no absolute moral standards. Therefore we can never trust them. Their dialogue is a farce. Therefore we cannot compromise and we cannot lie. We cannot deceive. Even the scope of co-operation is very limited. Truth will win in the end. God's Kingdom is coming. And no system that establishes itself on the basis of persecution and concentration camps and sacrifice of human man is compatible with Christianity which is based upon the supreme sacrifice of the life of the Son of God. By the virtue of His life and death, He alone has the right to rule the world. Including China.

At the Berlin Congress on Evangelism back in 1966, I remember a statement made by Ted Engstrom. He said, "The great challenge confronting the Church today is to identify and to locate every person in the world by the end of this century." There is no individual, no people who cannot be reached with the Gospel if we set ourselves to this supreme task of the Church. We can truly go to every creature. Yet at Berlin, it was not permitted to say even one word about the Communist countries. God forbid that we should have another Congress here without getting deeply involved in what we're talking about. We love Him when we keep His commandments. We can do it, this evangelization of

China, if we believe and obey the Bible. But we cannot, if we seek excuses. One of the excuses I often hear is that the Chinese must do it. There were overseas Chinese at the time of Morrison and Taylor, too. And remember, there are only 30 million Chinese outside China but there are three billion other people outside China. You do not know what God can do. But don't limit God by any preconceived idea because by faith in Christ and by prayer to God, by obedience to the Holy Spirit, by courage, by determination, by supreme sacrifice, we can accomplish the task of evangelizing China in our generation.

The Bible is full of men and women of God who did the humanly impossible. They made themselves available to God. And He did not choose them on the basis of their own moral integrity. You only have to read Hebrews 11 to understand that. We need people who rigidly, courageously return to the Word of God as the sole basis of authority. And He said, "Go ye and no one can stop you." This is the only source of the message, and that is Jesus, our only guide. What they did, we can. What they suffered, we might. What they accomplished, we should too and what they did wrong we need not do wrong because we have them as an example. Let us restore the authority of the Word of God in our own lives such that it will bring about revival by the spiritual power of a minority. We'll bring back the fear of the Lord. It ends divisions. It ends backbiting and criticism. For we tremble at the Word and the Word forbids it. And no revolution or anarchy ever came, to my knowledge, to a country or nation where God's Word had a central place.

I remember something that George Young wrote in a book called "The Living Christ in Modern China." He spoke about scriptural evangelism. He said, "The evangelism that we practice must be that healthy, balanced evangelism of Jesus which seeks the salvation of the whole man — mind, body and soul. The revival that we pray for must be spiritual and social. It must go deep in cleansing the moral life and wide in transforming the social and economic life of our nation. It must be a revival of apostolic preaching and of apostolic practicing of Christianity." It is my deep personal conviction that the answer to the challenge of Communism is a return to apostolic Christianity, with a flaming evangelism, and a Kingdom of God community life that will be more revolutionary than that of the Communists. All of that is in the Word of God.

God is preparing us for China. Never have so many missions met focusing on China. In my travels around the world, I've never met so many people praying for China. And I know that whatever we do will truly depend on Almighty God. Recently, I have studied thousands of pages on this subject, most of them produced by mission-oriented organizations. They never mentioned prayer. Do we still think that we can fight a battle? Let's examine our own publications and practices to see whether prayer has the role and the reality it should have. S. D. Gordon wrote in his book, "Quiet Talks on Prayer," "Prayer opens a whole planet to a man's activities." If it can open planets, it can open China. When we know what we want and when we know what we want to do and when we know God, and when we are rightly related to Him through Jesus Christ, and then we pray, then God will speak. God will answer. God will show us what is to come.

So no workers should be taken by surprise as happened to many in Indo-China. God will show us what to do. God will give us a strategy. Since we know what is the Will of God, with His Church and with the role of the Church in this world of revolution, therefore, we can do some long-range planning. That applies particularly to the future of the young people here. But there's a price to be paid. I've already mentioned Mark 13, verse 10. The Gospel must first be preached to all nations. That verse is sandwiched between verse 9 and 11, providing us with a classic setting for the proclamation of the Gospel in today's oppressive world, the setting of the criminal court, the interrogation room and the concentration camp. That is where today tens of thousands of our fellow believers are paying the price of our liberty. They pay a tremendous price. If we are willing to pay that price too, then, there are no closed doors, because God has never closed the doors. He has sent us into all the world to all nations. Believe the Word of God and not the newspapers. Then, we'll get ready and we'll go, walking the way that God is showing us. Some may never come back. Some of my own friends today are in prison, sentenced to many years imprisonment. We, in Open Doors teams, have no guarantee in the Bible that we will always come back from a trip into Communist countries. This consideration should be the base of our further studies this week. Let's bow before the Lord.

Thank you, Lord Jesus, that you have gone all the way and that you have said, "Follow me." Now, give us the love that you have for China. Enable us to go to the cross and die. Teach us, Lord Jesus, how you want to do it today. Give us that quality of life that will challenge the entire world. Give us that love and unity among ourselves that will make the world take notice. Make us men and women of God for the sake of China. For the sake of the world. In Jesus Name. Amen.

Chapter 1

Christian Churches in China 1807-1949

By Arnold Lea

Romans 9:17, 18.

To Pharaoh He said, "I have raised you up for the very purpose of showing my power in you. So that my name may be proclaimed in all the earth."

God's Sovereignty is seen as follows:

1. God gave a burden and love for China to dedicated men of His own choosing.   1807-1842
2. God over-ruled the regrettable actions of foreign governments.   1842-1860
3. The missionary movement grew and thus the Church grew also.   1860-1900
4. The implications of anti-foreign and anti-Christian attitudes were serious.   1900-1930

5. Chinese Christians were chosen
and prepared of God to bring
revival to His Church.   1930-1937

6. Christians were tested during
the Sino-Japanese war.   1937-1945

7. God prepared the Church for
the era of antagonistic
atheism.   1945-1949

I have been asked to interpret history and
find what we learned, what we could have
learned and what we have failed to learn.

I am going to present seven salient points
that come in the period under review and seek
to show the Sovereignty of God over-ruling the
affairs and the actions of men. The divisions are
purely arbitrary but are used as they illustrate
the main interpretation that the God of history
— of all history — is sovereign, the absolute
sovereign, King of Kings and Lord of Lords. He
raises up His Pharaohs and He disposes of them
at will, allowing them first to fulfill His purposes; yes, sometimes by their unrighteous
deeds.

1. GOD GAVE A BURDEN AND LOVE FOR CHINA TO DEDICATED MEN OF HIS OWN CHOOSING. 1807-1842.

Prior to the period under review,
Nestorians, Franciscans and Jesuits had sought
to bring Christianity to China with varying
degrees of success. Robert Morrison was the first

post-Reformation Protestant to bring the Gospel to China. He arrived in 1807 but like several others was unable to gain a foothold on the Mainland. They found ways of working for China. Some lived in Bangkok, some in Malaysia, and some, like Morrison, in Macau. One of them, Karil Gutzlaff, visited along the China coast but similarly failed to obtain permission to stay permanently. This closed door did not deter them from their efforts, and we thank God that He chose men of such determination to plant the Church in China. Though for the most part without educational privileges, they persevered. God chose men like Morrison for their spiritual gifts. Twelve long years were spent in Macau learning the language and that without modern aids. During that time he also translated the whole of the Bible into Chinese. He also preached and had to wait seven years before he baptized his first convert. What faith! What faith in the sovereignty of God, to continue preparing while the door to China remained for so long firmly closed.

2. GOD OVER-RULED THE REGRETTABLE ACTIONS OF FOREIGN GOVERNMENTS. 1842-1860.

Apart from an occasional move, the door to China remained closed for a long time. Missionaries sat on the perimeter, burdened, praying, working, but unable to take the message in. During that time the British government was involved in an effort to force opium upon the Chinese people, and eventually went to war concerning this and other matters of trading rights. At the end of this shameful opium war the Treaty of Nanking was signed in 1842. This opened five treaty ports along the coast of China to foreign businessmen, and incidentally allowed residence in China to the foreign missionary. Perhaps we find it difficult to reconcile that this should have been the way in which the door opened. But I can only accept the sovereignty of God which allows the independent and un-righteous acts of men to do things, which, though a blot on history, are yet used to work out for the furtherance of the Gospel. I feel I must underline this for unless we can see that God who has been sovereign throughout history is still sovereign over the affairs of men, then we are without a foundation for all our prayers and concern for the Church and for the people of China. The Psalmist has said, "Surely the wrath of men shall praise Him." Man's unrighteousness helped open the door of China to the planting of God's Church in that land.

In 1858 after further war with France and Great Britain, China was forced to sign yet another unequal treaty which opened a further ten cities to residence by foreigners, with per-mission to travel widely. Thus missionaries could proclaim the Gospel in the interior where hitherto the doors had been closed. Most famous of those itinerating missionary preachers was Dr. Griffith Jones of L.M.S. who made numerous trips from Hankow to neighbouring provinces. Others made arduous treks of months' duration to bring the Gospel to millions dying without Christ.

3. **THE MISSIONARY MOVEMENT GREW AND THUS THE CHURCH GREW ALSO. 1860-1900.**

Because this is inseparable from the results of their work, it is really a record of the growth of the Church. These years saw a phenomenal growth in missionary outreach from most western countries and from almost every kind of denominational background. By 1895 there were 41 missionary societies with a total of 1,300 missionaries, half of whom belonged to the China Inland Mission, formed only 30 years before by Hudson Taylor.

The variety of missions, denominational and otherwise, led naturally to the establishment of varied patterns of Church government. We could well wish now that churches planted then would have been more indigenous in culture and forms of worship, but at that time such concepts were rare and eagerness to have results led to the reproduction of western forms and western divisions. There can be no doubt about the self-sacrificing spirit of the pioneer missionaries nor of their compassion for those who suffered.

Their photo albums would indicate that they were often moved to pity by human suffering as much as by spiritual need. Their compassion for those that suffered may have led them to minister more to the poor, the sick, and the suffering than to aim in the higher strata of society and seek out men who would be leaders. There are all too few cases recorded of those who made close friendships with the scholars of those days resulting in their conversion to Christianity. Considering how hard it was to become a Christian, it is a cause of praise to God that at this stage there were already over 80,000 church members in China.

During this period a Chinese missionary society was formed in San Francisco in 1884 and missionaries sent to Kwangtung Province. I have been unable to trace records of the result of their work, but I think this must be the first Chinese missionary society brought into existence.

One of the lessons that emerges is that of identification. Hudson Taylor and others sought in their generation to express this by mode of dress, by way of life, by simplicity of accommodation. And where there was identification and integration, there was acceptance and following. Now, I want to use this as a lesson. Whatever may be our hope for making a contribution to China, whether we are Chinese or whether we are sympathetic people of other races, unless we can identify with 800 million people in their thought patterns, and in their problems, and in their difficulties, I wonder if we are going to get very far. We have a glorious Gospel to preach and nothing shall change our Gospel. But we must surely understand in some way what it means for them to be in the situation they are. And it is essential for us, in our prayers and in our thoughts and in our attitudes and in our hearts, to identify with them. Failing this, I think we shall fail. Now, the fourth point I want to make, and it has been touched on already, is the implication of the anti-foreign and the anti-Christian attitudes and the lessons that we must see from them, and how we see, once again, that God is sovereign.

4. THE IMPLICATIONS OF ANTI-FOREIGN AND ANTI-CHRISTIAN ATTITUDES WERE SERIOUS. 1900-1930.

As China became stronger among the nations, it was not surprising that anti-foreign attitudes should spring up, and combined with them and possibly linked to them, — this is something I want to underline — there were anti-Christian feelings. The year 1900 saw the outbreak of the notorious Boxer Movement, the Boxer Rebellion. One hundred and eighty-nine missionaries and their children were put to death. But it is very seldom recorded that a far, far greater number of Chinese Christians were put to death. The figure I have seen has been put as high as 16,000. Far more devastating, but less written about. They suffered rather than deny their faith. I cannot help wondering whether the motives of putting them to death was solely because of their adherence to Christ. Surely not. Surely, it was because they were associated, in the mind of their slayers, with foreigners and with their religion. I feel we need to think very deeply about the effects of relationships between those of different races.

God continued to bless and there seemed to be a fluctuation between times of deep persecution and times when Christianity almost became popular, such as during the revolution of Dr. Sun Yat Sen and following it, 1911, and after. Christianity became popular because that revolution was not anti-foreign. It was therefore not anti-Christian and the Church flourished. Dr. Latourette's writing in this period, in Volume III of *Christianity and the Revolution Aid* says, "Christianity began to fill the vacuum. Confucianism was disappearing. Buddhism was weak. Taoism was almost on the verge of dying and Animism could not hope to flourish in the secular age being ushered in." That was written forty years ago about a situation forty years earlier. However, the number of Protestant baptisms rose rapidly, and if we include the number of those who were adherents, it had risen from 80,000 to 800,000. Especially in the last five years before 1949 it rose by about forty percent. Thus had the Christian workers become attached to the Church.

There was great growth in Christian colleges and schools, in the distribution of literature, in Bible translation, and above all, in incentives of medical training. However, back in 1922 and then on to 1927, there were increasing signs of anti-foreign and anti-Christian attitudes. In 1927 another wave of persecution brought all the missionaries to the coast. It was during that time that they themselves discussed the emphasis on the three selves: self-government, self-support and self-propagation. When these were promulgated, alas, many missionaries and some Chinese leaders found it difficult to accept them, especially in view of the rapid turnover. In their enthusiasm, I think, the churches and the missionaries moved sometimes too quickly, and in other places they were very much too slow. But I want to emphasize that this was the beginning of the three self movements, and we should not confuse it with that which was introduced later in the 1950's, under the pressure of local authorities, as a means of bringing the Church under the control of the government. Personally, I can look back to 1933 to see real pressure being brought even in the interior to move towards self-support and self-government and self-propagation. But it was often very mysteriously misunderstood. Some missionaries in their enthusiasm would sit back so much, that they were referred to as just "home-sitters" or "guests" in the country rather than fellow-workers. But we see the fluctuation depending on whether there were anti-foreign or anti-Christian attitudes. I feel we want, if possible, to learn a lesson for the future.

Possibly one outstanding lesson concerns what part we foreigners should play in any movement that missionaries might help in. I feel that unless the presence and participation of those of us from other races can be satisfactorily explained and appreciated, this very presence could hinder Chinese from proclaiming the Gospel as universal and not somehow tainted.

Racial chauvinism is so deeply imbedded in people's attitudes, that if there is someone from another race around, we assume our religion comes from that place. I feel that we must, in our thinking and in our burden and in our prayer, be willing perhaps even to fulfill the will of God by our absence.

This is going to need prayerful consideration. How may we participate and share our burden and yet not prejudice the situation? I feel that it is something that each one of us needs prayerfully to consider now, long before any possible situation arises. In some situations our very absence may be in the interest of God's Kingdom.

5. CHINESE CHRISTIANS WERE CHOSEN AND PREPARED OF GOD TO BRING REVIVAL TO THE CHURCH. 1930-1939.

This is the time when God, in His Sovereign Grace, gave gifts to the Church. He chose and prepared men of God, Chinese men of God, to bring revival to the Church. During these ten years, it seemed in a special way that God raised up a group of men and a diversity of gifts, for He was moving on in His purpose for the Church in China. There had previously been men with outstanding gifts, of course. But not to the extent, numerically, or in a nationwide influence that seems to have happened in this decade we are thinking of. Of course, outstanding is Dr. Sung Sang Tie. He used to bring revivals to practically every province of China and every country in Southeast Asia. In a new way, he preached sin. I can't explain it, except as I experienced something of this movement myself. Previously, people had preached that men were sinners, but they had not preached sin specifically. God gave this man a mighty burden and a great gift. Everywhere he went, as we all know so well, there was personal conviction of sin. Not group conviction, but personal conviction of sin. There were tears and there was repentance, resulting in new life. It even happened to missionaries and it was interesting that many of our Chinese colleagues said to us, "You've been born again." Life came because of conviction. To this day, there are amongst us, men and women who had their spiritual reviving through Dr. Sung. It lasted. God did something for the Church in China then. And he had an emphasis on lay preaching then, as we know. It reminds us that long, long before the present emphasis on verbalizing the laity, Dr. John Sung had had this vision from God. It's no new concept. God, through him, sent out hundreds, thousands of laymen to preach the Gospel. The Bethel Bands followed under the leadership of Pastor Gih Chi Wen, Andrew Gih. They were a phenomenon of the early and latter 1930's. They went everywhere bring blessing, not only into coastal provinces, but into the hinterland of China.

Then there was Watchman Nee, Mr. Nee To Chen, versed in the Scriptures, who brought to the Church of God a new challenge to go into a deeper life with God, and incidentally, whose writings challenged people to think through again the pattern of Church order generally and the pattern of their own Church. In Kiangsi, God raised up another man, not so well known personally, for he didn't travel so widely, Yung Ch'ao-t'ang. But he has been appreciated, through his teachings on the pattern for the local Church, a book which permeated into the hinterlands and into the smaller villages even of China. Incidentally, when he was working, he introduced into his work the Ling Kwang Tan of the spiritual worker teams he initiated. What some feel as only now a modern concept in service training, was known then. God had given him a vision. He not only trained Chinese but he trained missionaries as they worked together in a fellowship. Dr. Jao Yu-ming is another whom God raised up before that time. But during that time, he had a very wide ministry, a conference ministry. He was also to be the father of a particular pattern of Ling Su Sio Yan, of spiritual training centers, which prepared many people of varied academic standards for fulltime service. It was a vision that came to him.

There was Mr. Wang Ming-tao, whose courageous stand and teaching during the Japanese War was a challenge to many. There were many others. But I doubt if, before that, and I doubt if, after that, God has, in quite such a way, given to His Church such a wealth of gifts as He did in these men and many others whose names I haven't mentioned. It was a time of reviving amongst missionaries also. When we sought to know where we were falling down and where we were out of touch with God, speaking personally, I cannot help but feel that we've failed the Church in placing too little emphasis on the responsibility of the laymen, almost an absence of emphasis on the Great Commission. I say it with shame as I stand before you. I don't remember, ever, during those years, challenging a young Chinese to go abroad as a missionary.

We were too concerned with the local Church and its needs instead of realizing that if the local Church, weak as it was, could have sent, it would have reaped the harvest.

But missions were not completely overlooked. One emphasis that caught the imagination was the Back to Jerusalem Band. Its purpose was that Chinese should move from China back through Central Asia, back to the place where on the day of Pentecost the Church was born. It was a vision given to a young man in Northwest China. And I wonder whether one day the Back to Jerusalem Band will not be once again formed, that there will go out from China a band which will visit not just Chinese but other inhabitants of Central Asia and, indeed, the world. This was the vision that we failed to give in those days.

6. CHRISTIANS WERE TESTED DURING THE SINO-JAPANESE WAR. 1937-1945.

Here's another period from 1937-1945, when God in His sovereign grace allowed a tremendous calamity to come to China and yet, through it, did something for His Church which possibly nothing else could have done. Under the invasion of the Japanese, the Chinese people suffered greatly. But during that time, God worked in many hearts and in many churches, preparing for greater suffering to come. Refugees who fled from the Japanese in the coastal provinces found the standards and methods of living in the north and west of China very different from the comparative ease of their homes in east China. They marveled that people in the west could put up with so few amenities. Many of those who fled, did so with little caution, with few possessions. On arrival, some would sell their wedding rings and begin a little wayside store. But it was the students who suffered much, suffered bitterness if anybody ever did. Poor food and damp, crowded conditions produced the high incidence of TB. Under these adverse conditions, to which the constant bombings of the Japanese planes were added sufferings, there came new spiritual dimensions to the Chinese Church. This is my interpretation of those years: a new spiritual dimension.

For one thing new environments meant a radical break with the past, including much unhealthy missionary control. The deeper spiritual experience of the Christians from eastern China came as a challenge to the rather less mature Christians of western China. The Church there had always been small, undeveloped and less dedicated. It received a completely new shot in the arm. But more wonderful was the fact that thousands of refugees themselves, who were not Christians during those days, found the reality of Christ. Thus, during the privations of the war with Japan, the Church grew and the lives of thousands were enriched. That was Church growth, certainly. Churches sprung up all over the big cities and out into the country as well, where God was raising up men and women to serve and lead the Church. The greatest response was amongst the middle school and university students. They not only found Christ but they were moved by the Holy Spirit to a dedication of their lives to God, which resulted in aggressive evangelism. Fervent and prolonged prayer meetings and a hunger for the Word of God, long, long nights of prayer were not uncommon by any means. And if you went to a student conference, from before dawn until well after midnight you could hear the sound of prayer coming over the hillside. It never seemed to cease, singly and in groups. There was a tremendous emphasis on prayer because prayer was the basis for witness in those days. Christians of those war years knelt and prayed. The students thought nothing of kneeling on the damp mud floors for hours. Such was their intensity and their dedication. There were no kneeling mats in those days. Earnestness was the order of the day and sometimes their prayer meetings could be heard as far as a quarter of a mile away on the campus. There was no hiding of a light under a bushel. No wonder the Church flourished. Privation produced reality.

The lesson we might well learn from this, "that in suffering, God does a mighty and a deep plan.

7. GOD PREPARED THE CHURCH FOR THE ERA OF ANTAGONISTIC ATHEISM. 1945-1949.

When we shall see that God was making His preparation, I cannot but mention that I feel very strongly that we, as missionaries, and as Church leaders and missionaries alike, made inadequate and unrealistic preparations for this antagonistic atheism which was to come. The writing was on the wall for any who were awake enough to read it. Yet there was an easy optimism. The laity thought that things would continue as they had been, or at any rate, after a change for a short time, they would return to normal. Reality only came when it was too late to prepare. But God was preparing. Thank God, *He* was realistic. The work amongst students had gathered such momentum that during the war years, that is in 1945, it was possible to call a conference in Chunking, convened under the leadership of Pastor Tao Chung Yin. Students came from all over China. Two hundred of them met for what was the first inter-university conference. There was heart searching, there was much prayer. I wish I could convey to you something of the spirit of that conference. There was deep repentance, there was utter dedication. The conference ended with a four-hour testimony meeting. And many people hadn't finished. We had to give our testimonies in unison after that. At any rate, we brought it to God whether our neighbor heard it or not, and we held hands and we cried out in worship and praise for what God had done, what the Sovereign Lord had done in the midst of the Japanese invasion. Tears were streaming down our faces, as we saw His mighty works. The spontaneity and the fervor was beyond description. Never before had two hundred voices been raised in praise. Over two hundred people went back to take the torch to their universities. Back in Nanking two years later, a larger student conference met, again, amidst scenes of fervor and enthusiasm, dedication and sacrifice, which I have not met since. I long for those days when the Spirit of God was moving in such evident ways. It was already there, a sense of God's purpose for the dark years to follow. And when the change of government came in '49, it was these ardent students who witnessed to a Godless regime. Thus, we see that in 1949, God prepared young men and women who loved not their lives to the death.

Not long ago, we were praying, my wife and I, for many of our colleagues of those days by name. And as we prayed we were visualizing them still as young men and women, as we had been separated from them. And we suddenly realized the passage of time. If they were alive today, they would be 45 or 50 years old. Their children would be grown up and probably married. Their grandchildren would be at an age when children who are free to do so rejoice to hear of the love of Jesus. May we be conscious of the passing of time but may we also be conscious of the Sovereignty of God whose thoughts do not run slow.

Chapter 2

China's Indigenous Christian Movements

By Rev. Princeton Hsu

My topic is the building up of the indigenous Chinese Church. We all know Christianity was first brought to China in modern times in 1807, when Rev. Morrison came to the Chinese coast. Hence, it has been almost 170 years since Christianity was brought to China. During these 170 years progress has been slow. Rev. Morrison worked 7 years before he won his first convert. He baptized him in Macau. In 1832, 25 years after Rev. Morrison arrived, there were only 10 Christians in China. By 1877, the number had increased slowly to just 13,000. In 1949, when big political changes took place in the Mainland, there were only 700 to 800 thousand Christians in China. Compared to other countries, the progress of evangelism has been very slow. What is the reason, many ask? Buddhism is also a foreign religion coming from India to China as Christianity came from the West. When Buddhism was brought to China, there were no mission boards or missionaries. Neither did they have any collections for sending out Buddhist missionaries. Even so, it took only a hundred odd years to convert the majority of the Chinese people. Soon Buddhism had become a Chinese religion. On the other hand, Christianity has set up mission boards, and has sent out many missionaries and spent large sums of money. Still, Christianity has spread much more slowly than Buddhism. Why? We all love Jesus. We all feel the urgency to evangelize China. This is a big question. There seem to be three reasons.

First, among all the religions of the world, Christianity is the hardest to propagate. As servants of God, we need to realize this fact and not be discouraged. Buddhism is full of superstitions which are easily accepted by man who is naturally superstitious. Confucianism is also easily accepted because it describes man as naturally good and kind. Sin and wrongdoing are due to one's lack of education or having the wrong kind of friends. Sin is the result of one's circumstances. This idea makes everybody happy and so is accepted. Christianity is different. It declares that whoever you are, however high a status you have, you are still a sinner bound for hell, if you do not believe in Christ. No one likes to hear this. We must recognize this fact and yet in spite of it, we have to spread the good news. So the first reason why Christianity spreads so slowly is that Christianity proclaims that all have sinned.

Secondly, it was particularly hard for the educated to accept Christianity. In the 19th century, when the missionaries came with their faith and their Bibles, many Western countries were also contemplating invading and dividing up China among themselves. It is obvious that the attitudes of these foreign governments affected the image of Christianity greatly. This kind of imperialistic attitude is never taught in the Bible but many foreign governments made use of religion to accomplish their own purposes. In the 19th century, in the 60 years after the Opium War, the history of evangelism in China was very sad. The people were confused by the fact that foreigners came, some carrying Bibles and others carrying guns. The people did not understand that this was not a true reflection of Christianity. Therefore, during these 60 years, 1840-1900, opposition to the Gospel was very strong. In fact, the outbreak of the Boxer Movement was aimed at creating antagonism to Christianity, to make people despise Christianity and Westerners as well. This caused great damage to Christianity, and is the second reason for slow progress.

The third reason was the lack of indigenousness in the Church during the period 1841-1900. The western style was maintained. Buddhism is different from Christianity in this regard.

It soon became Chinese and made the people feel as if it was something of their own. On the other hand Christianity was considered as a Western religion and Jesus Christ was not someone for the Chinese people. The progress of the indigenous movement in the Chinese churches has been very slow and this constitutes the third reason for the slow rate of evangelism. Even today, in Shanghai or Peking, the Christian's Easter is called the "Western Memorial Day," and Christmas is the "Western Winter Festival." So it is obvious that people still regard Christianity as foreign.

Today we want to look at the history of the indigenous movement in the Chinese church. We ought to thank God for showing us the importance of indigenousness without which Christianity cannot take root in China. The history began in 1900, after the Boxer Movement, when changes began to take place in the Church. In 1902-1903, a wave of independent movements began in Canton City where the first Independent Chinese Church — the Canton Hsin-Wah Independent Baptist Church was established. It was supported totally by the Chinese congregation without any foreign aid. In 1906, Brother Yiu Chung Chou started another ICC in Shanghai. Then in 1924 came an official call for the first time for three autonomous actions: self-dependence, self-support and self-propagation. Another important date is 1926, when the foreign mission boards of the Presbyterian, Anglican and Baptist Churches handed over all their churches' properties to the Chinese. They said, "We will let you Chinese take over and we will only be consultants and helpers." Thank you Lord. Ever since 1926, Jesus Christ has been much glorified. It was 1929 when the Indigenous Movement was first mentioned and the action started. Thank God for the step-by-step guidance. In the book *The Building of the Chinese Indigenous Church*, pages 8 and 10 tell of the historical details of the whole movement. These are all my personal experiences. I was born in 1900 in Shanghai and lived there for most of my life, and therefore witnessed all these happenings and the guidance of God. We truly thank our heavenly Father for all His love for China, for the Chinese Church, for the Chinese Christians and thank God for His blessings. I am not going to talk about the historical facts which you can learn by reading the book.

Rather, I will discuss the concept of indigenousness. In 1929 when the call for indigenousness was made, many became very excited. Some suggested that Buddhist ceremonies should be used in the Sunday worship. Others suggested that Chinese music, Chinese melody, Chinese musical instruments should be used. Still others suggested that in the Holy Communion Chinese foods should be

served. They thought that this was indigenousness. Some Western missionaries even agreed to
build a Church resembling a temple. I won't
discuss these examples for they may have their
points, though sometimes things were overdone.
It depends on the circumstances. At the time
there were some who disagreed with the idea of
changing the outward forms and suggested that
it was an indigenous Chinese theology which
could solve the basic problem. This is reasonable
and there were calls for pure Chinese seminaries
and ministerial work.

What is an indigenous Chinese Church?
Dear co-workers, and fellow-believers, I would
like you each to spend time considering this
question. Is it the inclusion of Chinese culture?
Is it to be self-dependence, self-support and self-
propagation? These are very superficial things. A
real indigenous church is not an American-style
or an English-style church. Rather it should be
patterned after the Biblical example. We can
find many mixtures in the Bible which are also
advocated in age-old Chinese culture. There are
many Chinese teachings which do not have any
conflict with Biblical commands either. For
example, respect and love for parents. Both
Israel and China surpass other nations in this
respect. China is a long-lived nation because we
Chinese love and respect our parents. This is to
be preserved and developed in Christianity. If we
want to have an indigenous Church, we have to

practice this towards our parents, so that Chinese can feel that this is a Chinese religion. Therefore, we ought to ponder over these questions to find out what real indigenousness is. But we should not get entangled in changes of forms which could pull us even farther away from real indigenousness. We ought to be careful.

Secondly, to be indigenous, it is essential to have a good testimony. Christianity does not stand without a testimony. By the same token we ought to remember our Christian righteousness when we preach the Gospel either to those inside the Mainland or to those overseas. If our righteousness does not exceed the righteousness of Buddhism, of Confucianism, we have no way to enter the Kingdom of God. Our testimony has to be better than theirs. The need is not new methods of reaching out but a "new person." The new person in Jesus Christ. A new method is not very useful. In the whole Bible from Genesis to Revelation, I cannot find any mention of new methods except by the son of King Solomon. He did not listen to his father and used new methods which caused divisions among the nation. Other than that, the Bible only mentions the need of a "new person" and a "new life." This is the most important point. Therefore, we need not new methods but new living testimonies.

Thirty years ago, there was a well-known

missionary who went to India intending to convert the Indians to Christ. Dr. Ghandi invited him to dinner and asked him what kind of method he was going to use to achieve his goal. Before he replied, Dr. Ghandi gave the answer saying, "It is most important that each of you Christians should reveal the image of Christ. Then India will be converted very quickly. However, if you do not practise what you preach, India will never be converted." He was right. What we need now is a living testimony. If we manifest the fragrance of Christ, China will be converted very quickly. Thank God, this is an important principle of the indigenous movement.

Lastly, one may ask, "According to what you have just said, are we badly indebted to God?" For a hundred and seventy years of the history of the Chinese Church, there are still not too many converts among the millions of Chinese spreading all over the world. Many are discouraged. Dear co-workers, and fellow-believers, do not be discouraged. Why? There are two reasons. First of all, if a religion is easily accepted, this religion is not genuine. A true one, even though preached widely, will still not be accepted by very many. If a religion has never been persecuted, that religion is not genuine. A true one will suffer persecution everywhere it is proclaimed, because everyone on earth who does not believe in Jesus Christ, is the enemy of God.

He prefers Satan to Christ. Christianity is the only truth and is persecuted everywhere, proving the genuineness of the faith. Secondly, in the past 170 years both missionaries and Chinese Christian workers have gained great accomplishment by laboring earnestly for Christ. It is quality but not quantity that counts in Christianity. We can see that Chinese Christians have had great influence in the past 170 years. The Bible tells us that each of us can chase a thousand men.

Chapter 3

The Chinese Christian Church under Communism 1949-1966

By Leslie Lyall

I want to begin by quoting those tremendous, victorious and reassuring words of our Lord to Peter concerning His Church in Matt. 16:18, words which should never be far from our thoughts in these days. Jesus said to Peter, "I will build my Church and the powers of hell shall not prevail against it." This alone is our confidence in thinking of the Church in China today and tomorrow.

My task is to portray the experience of the Christian Church in China from the institution of the People's Republic in 1949 up to the Great Proletarian Cultural Revolution in 1966. I do not propose to repeat what I have written in *Come Wind, Come Weather* and *Red Sky at Night*. But I must try, in the light of what we now know, to make an objective assessment of those events. This is a task of great difficulty but also one of the greatest importance, not only for our own proper understanding of what

39

the Chinese Church was called to pass through but also for the sake of every other Church in the world today which may, sooner or later, be called to face a similar ordeal. I am glad to know that *Come Wind, Come Weather,* translated into a number of foreign languages has been widely used in Africa, Latin America and in Asia as a textbook for the study of Communist tactics in relation to the Church. And I have no doubt that the findings of this seminar will prove to be of even greater value for the same purpose, will be read by Church leaders all over the world. That is why we must seek to discover the truth about China, divorced from mere propaganda, either of the right or of the left. That truth must be firmly based on a foundation of demonstratable threat and not merely on sweeping and optimistic generalizations which in turn rely on the flimsy framework of isolated incidents, a few case histories, occasional letters and reports of refugees and travellers in China. This can only distort the true overall picture of the actual situation for the Church in China as a whole. And let us honestly confess that the sum total of all our information is very limited indeed.

May I be allowed first of all to recapitulate the substance of earlier papers and also to remind all those what kind of a Church the Protestant Church in China was in 1949. This is very important in the light of subsequent events.

First of all, it was a Church with a short history. About 115-117 years back to Morrison. But as a living Church, about 115 years compared with a thousand years of history in Russia. Secondly, it was a numerically small Church totalling about one million or .2 percent of the population. Thirdly, it was a theologically mixed Church with the official organizations dominated by liberal theology. Fourthly, it was a spiritually alive Church which had experienced Revival Movement at each decade of the present century. Fifthly, it was largely an autonomous Church, organizationally and financially independent of western control and finance. Sixthly, it was a maturely led Church. There have been many well-trained, able and spiritually minded men and women in all sections of the Church. Seventhly, it was an ill-prepared Church as far as being able to face the confrontation where Marxist ideology was concerned.

The main difficulty this Church had to face in 1949 was first of all, an atheistic ideology which regards all religion as unscientific superstition and therefore, an error to be vigorously opposed; secondly, the history of Christian missions in China, which can be so interpreted as to support the notion that the Chinese Churches have always been a tool of imperialism; and thirdly, the Chinese Church's apparent support of the previous so-called reactionary regime and the Church's failure to participate in any radical

41

social reforms. So much for the background.

Our first consideration must be the Christian Manifesto. In December, 1949, nineteen Chinese Christian leaders addressed a long message to the Boards of the Missions they represented. They clearly stated their belief in the disinterested courage of foreign missions, but recognized that there must come a change in the Church's relationship with the older Churches and with Chinese society. The churches had waited for the communist take-over with fear and foreboding in spite of official communist assurances of religious freedom. But when in May, 1950 several "Church of Christ in China" — that is the official body — leaders were invited to Peking for a three-day conference with Mr. Chou En-lai, the Premier, many Christians felt themselves honored. The outcome of the conference was a document called "The Christian Manifesto," which, while opening with an expression of appreciation of Christianity's contribution to China, went on to state the terms under which the Protestant Church could hope to survive in the New China. These terms were a required admission of the way in which the Church had allegedly been used as a tool of imperialist designs on China, and specified a determination to free itself of all imperialist influences. The Church also pledged its allegiance to the People's Government and agreed to maintain absolute obedience to the Communist

Party. Only the Anglican Church, among the major denominations, refused to sign the document and published one of its own. But eighty thousand people, including 1,527 Chinese leaders, did sign the Manifesto. The immediate effect of the Manifesto published in August, 1950 was the withdrawal of all foreign protestant missions from the Chinese Mainland. Thus, the Manifesto was the first test of strength of the Chinese Church in relation to the State. It's easy to say now that these Christian leaders should never have accepted the fundamental thesis of the Manifesto, and that in doing so, they betrayed the missionary movement which had given birth to the Church by consenting to enforce the Manifesto, thereby placing a powerful weapon in the hands of the Church's enemies. Only those present during those three fateful days in Peking know whether in fact there was any protest against the terms or any resistance to the clear intention of the government. But those Christian leaders must have believed that they were being presented with an ultimatum and that there was no alternative to submission. Survival itself seemed to be at stake. In itself, the Manifesto did not obviously constitute a breach of any Biblical principle although its implications were far-reaching. We, today, would be wise to take note of the way in which the very concept of the term missionary has been denigrated in China. And for what reasons. And we should ask ourselves if there is someway of avoiding the use of that term at least in speaking of the future of the Christian witness in China.

I turn to the Three Self Patriotic Movement. At an early date the People's Government created a ministry of religion, having separate departments to deal with each religious group in particular. During the land reform period in 1950 many rural Churches were temporarily closed. But in 1951 to '52, they were reopened and the congregations were ordered to reassemble. In April, 1951, 158 Christian leaders met in Peking, officially, to dispose of missionary property, to sever relations with U.S. imperialism, and to promote full indigenization. One important outcome was the launching of the "Oppose America Aid Korea," Three Self Reform Movement of the "Church of Christ in China" that being rather a mouthful, they expressed it more briefly as the Three Self Reform Church. The slogan "love country, love Church" was adopted. By the end of 1951, the Church in China was totally isolated from all outside relationships. Immediately, Christian ministers were required to become self or state employed. Sermons were vetoed, baptisms restricted and all Christian activity confined to Church buildings. All Christian schools, hospitals and charitable welfare institutions were taken out of Church control. Large sums of money were also allocated for the re-education of the clergy. In 1954, Mr. Wai Ching-wu, president of the movement, reviewing the first four years at a national conference in Peking, claimed that there was a greater spiritual unity than ever before. By that time, no branch of the Christian Church had been able to remain outside the movement. Even the early dissenters had fallen into line. Both the Little Flock and the True Jesus Church, the two largest independent Churches, with other such groups, were now formally represented. Mr. Wu declared that loyalty to and love for the Church on the part of Christians were unchanged. But his address also perpetuated the notion that the entire missionary movement had been a tool of imperialist aggression against China. In one of the meetings, however, the objection was raised to the use of the word "reform" by those who feared its possible theological implications chiefly, the independent Little Flock and the Ling Liang T'ang. The term was therefore changed and the organization became known as the Chinese Christian Three Self Patriotic Movement.

In 1956, two hundred and sixty nine delegates in every province attended a third national conference in Peking. The following year witnessed The Hundred Flowers episode. Amidst the sudden gush of open criticism of the government, the Rev. Marcus Chang, Vice-

45

President of the Three Self Patriotic Movement,
had one of five Christians appointed to the
People's Political Consultative Council, the
equivalent of a Parliament or House of Repre-
sentatives, launch an outspoken attack in that
Assembly on the government for its failure to
respect the sensitivities of Christians and to
maintain a Constitutional respect for religion. It
was an act of great courage. During the Chinese
New Year of 1958, all the pastors were gathered
for political training and a strong attack was
launched on miraculous effects. In the same
year, arguing that denominations were a
missionary device to facilitate the foreign
domination of the Churches, the Religious
Affairs Bureau ordered the Churches to take
steps to unite. Many Church buildings were con-
sequently closed, notably in Shanghai and
Peking. The movement celebrated its 10th
anniversary in 1959 with parades in many cities.
It claimed to have reached maturity. The fourth
national conference of the movement was held
in Shanghai in 1960 when a spokesman said that
the counter-revolutionary ring of Watchman Nee
and Wang Ming-tao had been broken up, that
most of the reactionary forces had been cleared
from the Churches. From that time on, the committee of the Three Self Movement, in face of
growing hostility to the Church, was drawn
increasingly into political activity in order to demonstrate its solidarity with the Chinese people.

Following a full-scale press attack on all religions in 1964, the Cultural Revolution of 1966 finally brought to an end all organized Church life. Not even the government-sponsored Three Self Movement could protect the Church from the violence of the Red Guards, so that even the most conformist of its leaders suffered indignity and humiliation along with the rest.

It's impossible to maintain that the Three Self Movement was a spontaneous creation of the Church itself. It was manifestly a creation of the government and resulted in the wedding of the Church to a secular state. It's easy for us now to denounce the Three Self Patriotic Movement as a Communist device to dominate and enslave the Church. In the mind of the government, it was clearly intended to achieve just that. But before condemning as compromises our brethren who bowed to the inevitable, we should consider several factors. Take Russia as a comparative case.

The Church in Russia had a thousand years of history behind it. The problems of Church and state relations had been worked out over a long period of time. And so the Church in Russia was in a good position to meet the new Communist forces when they came into power. Those of you who know and read about the Church in Russia will appreciate what I'm saying. The Chinese Church on the contrary was comparatively young, and it never had to concern itself much with Church-state relationships. It has been largely left alone to conduct its own affairs without State interference. Thus, it was quite unprepared to meet the demands of the State. How did the teaching of Scripture apply to this new situation?

Views on this issue differ. Some initially opposed state control, vigorously and courageously. Others, joining and believing probably in Romans 13, equally conscientous, felt it right to cooperate. They included such evangelical stewards as the Rev. Marcus Chang and the Rev. Young Shao-tang. Secondly, in East Germany, the Christian Church with its long history since the Reformation, its Lutheran principles about Church-state relationships and its opposition to Hitler, had given its moral and practical support to the social and economic policies of the German Democratic Republic without compromising its theological convictions. Is there any ground therefore for criticizing the Church in China for following the Germany example and for supporting the social and economic reforms which, as old impartial observers admit, have already achieved much materially and morally for the common people of China? Thirdly, in an authoritarian State, it is impossible to conceal any institution or organization outside the control of State. It is, therefore, academic to discuss whether or not the Three Self Movement was something spontaneous or a government device to control the Church.

That the Church as an institution would be under State control was inescapable. There was no alternative except to go underground. For this, the Chinese Church was at that time simply not prepared. Since the Cultural Revolution of 1966-1969, the Church in China has been described as an institutionless community of the redeemed. Even the Three Self Movement no longer functions although it remains on the list of national institutions. Possibly the Church will never again function as an institution under State control. It may be better that it should not do so. But we must also ask ourselves whether the Church in China can in the future function at all effectively without some sort of structure, however informal. Or should it again seek to reascertain to assert its constitutional rights to the freedoms promised?

I now turn to the controversial question of the human cost of Communism for China as a whole and for the Church in particular. And here, we must try to sift the charges of anti-communist propaganda from the ascertainable facts. The precise statistics will never be known. We are not here concerned with the terrible loss of life on both sides prior to 1949 in one of the bloodiest civil wars in history. The years 1950 to 1952 were the years of terror when all over China landlords, capitalists, counter-revolutionaries and spies faced peoples' courts which con-

49

demned them to die during a series of political
campaigns. In a speech in 1959, Chairman Mao
gave the figure of those liquidated as 800,000.
In the mid 1950's an official Chinese communist
figure quoted by the East Asia Harvard Research
Center was 2.8 million. This figure approximates
to an estimate of three million made by a
Christian who emerged from China in 1972,
having been in many prominent positions and
who was in a good position to know. Some in
the West have speculated that the total figure
might be as many as 15 million. The figure of
Christian casualties was even more difficult to
estimate. Probably some Christians who were in
the above four categories lost their lives, but not
necessarily because they were Christians. During
the terror in 1951, when people were made the
objects of accusation, there were numerous
suicides including those of some Christians. But
persistent rumors reaching the West about the
deaths of certain leading Christians were later
shown to be false. Not even the leaders of the
so-called counter-revolutionary organizations,
Watchman Nee, Wang Ming-tao or their
followers suffered a death sentence. They were
condemned to long imprisonment but not to
death. The Roman Catholics fared far worse than the
Protestants. As many as 700 priests may have died in
prison or labor camps between 1952 and 1954. During
the Anti-Rightist campaign in 1958, one report

from China said "many are earning the crown of life." But Miss Helen Willis, who continued to live and work in Shanghai until 1959 knew nothing of any large scale execution of Christians. I know two well-informed and highly placed Chinese who left China in 1972 and in 1974. I have cross examined them both in great detail. So in my article on China in the new international dictionary of the Christian Church, I wrote that several hundred Chinese Christians may have lost their lives. And on the facts available, I stand by their figure while admitting that first information could necessitate a revision of the statement.

It is not a policy of the People's Government to kill off those who do not agree entirely with them, provided the dissenters are not class enemies and counter-revolutionary elements. The Christian Church has never been classified among the enemies of the State though it is regarded as reactionary. Contradictions among the people is a fact of life and welcome.

In Chairman Mao's famous essay on Contradictions, he wrote: "We cannot abolish religion by administrative decree or force people not to believe in it. We cannot compel people to give up idealism any more than we can force them to believe in Marxism. The only way to settle questions of an ideological nature or controversial issues among the people is by the democratic method, the method of discussion, of criticism, of persuasion and education and not by the method of coercion or repression." The Chinese leaders believed that religion does not need to be eliminated but it will wither away and in due course die a natural death as a consequence of a systematic education of the younger generation. This is not to say that imprisonment, solitary confinement, public accusations and torture have not been used in the process of persuasion and education. If the cost in terms of human life has been far short of some extravagant claims, the reality of persecution is beyond doubt.

In April 1951, the Peking Conference of the Three Self Movement launched its accusation campaign, beginning with six prominent Christians accused of being rightists. This campaign was rationalized by reference to our Lord's denunciation of the Pharisees. The whole nation was, at that time, in a grip of fear. Fear was also the weapon used in the accusation campaign because Christian leaders had to attend struggle meetings before their own congregations. These meetings were staged and managed by government cadres who conducted the fierce criticism of these leaders and demanded a complete and honest self criticism as well. Some moral skeletons in the cupboard were undoubtedly brought to light and given wide publicity in the national press. But the normal charges were those of being associated with missionaries and of accepting imperialism money. Many were sent to prison or slave labor camps. Hundreds were relieved of their pastorage, especially any who had been educated in the U.S.A. Such were assigned to perform menial and degrading tasks. Some, under these pressures, committed suicide while others went out of their minds. The purpose of this treatment were said to be reform, rebirth and reinstatement. After the purges were complete, individuals and Churches were admitted to the ranks of Reformed Churches. The mass denunciation by Christians of their fellow believers and spiritual leaders at that time is a tragic episode in the history of attempted accommodation to the powers within. Through 1955, mass accusation campaigns were conducted throughout China, chiefly against Mr. Wang Ming-tao, the Peking pastor, and a communist heretic by the name of Wu Fong. Wang Ming-tao was arrested in August and a wave of further arrests followed in September and October. The campaign against Wang Ming-tao was succeeded in 1955 by a virilant campaign against the Christian Assembly or of the Flock as many others know the name, whose leader, Watchman Nee, was already in prison. Thirty other leaders faced denunciation before 2,500 fellow Christians. By 1958, it was estimated that 80 percent of China's ordained ministers were without Churches and were working in factories or on farms. Conditions for Christians after 1958 amid the setting up of the communes grew steadily worse as hostility towards the Churches increased. In 1964, the national press launched a full-scale attack on all religion. And finally, in 1966, the Three Self Movement itself crumbled under the Red Guard offensive. This proved to be the fiercest attack yet on the Church. Church leaders were humiliated and often physically maltreated. Some were sent to correction camps and others, once again, chose suicide as a way out. Everywhere, Christians suffered great hardships. By Easter 1967, the liquidation of the organized Church was complete.

But one thing has become crystal clear: that even this furious climax, the 15 years of persecution, did not succeed in destroying the Church which Christ Himself said He would build. So, let us consider more briefly than I would choose, the Living Church in the midst of persecution. The period from 1949 to 1955 has been described as one of missions, conversions, baptisms and miracles. The official "Church of Christ in China," reported 18% growth in Church membership in the province of Chekiang, 22% in the province of Shantung and 30% in the area south of the Yangtze, known as Chiang-Nan, between 1953 and 1956. In the provinces of Anhwei and Hunan, Church membership increased by 2,000 and 3,000 respectively after the departure of the missionaries in 1951. The independent evangelical students who worked in Peking were not disbanded until 1955. And the students continued to hold annual conferences and frequent nights of prayer. Despite the nationwide accusation movement against Wang Ming-tao, this courageous warrior held the largest evangelistic mission of his life in 1955, in the capital city of communist China, and there were many conversions. In Shanghai, too, there were many conversions. And evangelical students held a conference there in 1954 attended by nine hundred. Chekiang reported six hundred baptisms between 1955 and 1960. Meanwhile, the youthful Chinese missionary societies such as the Chinese Evangelistic Band, the Back to Jerusalem Band and the Christian Workers Mission, continued their fruitful work along China's borders. Even Tibetans were turning to Christ.

The year 1956 was one of refreshing for many churches through revival meetings. The following year, some imprisoned Christians were released. In 1960, 146 men, women and students were attending theological colleges in Peking and Nanking. And one of the released leaders, who visited Shansi Province in 1961, reported the glorious progress of God's work in many lives, especially among the young. And his comment was, "in the past, the Church was building on sand. But now, it is being built on the rock." However, increasing pressures, especially in the larger cities, were forcing more and more Christians into small house groups. Jack Job of the Hongkong Standard reported — "the visible and formal Churches are dying out while the invisible formless non-political and true Churches are growing in numbers." Following the Red Guard campaign in 1966, Christians finally went under-ground.

From that time on, news of the Churches and the Christians became very scarce indeed and reliable news continues to be comparatively scarce even now. Our sources of information have always been confined to close-hand reports of Chinese visitors to China, the stories of refugees from China, possible letters from friends and relatives in China, and letters written to the Far East Broadcasting Company by listeners. Seeing that overseas Chinese living in Southeast Asia originate almost exclusively from Kwangtung, Fukien and Chekiang, these south-eastern provinces, together with Shanghai and Yunnan's border area are virtually the only parts of China from which we receive news. We are grateful to God for every scrap of good news we are receiving but we must avoid the temptation to make misleading generalizations on the basis of a limited knowledge of the situation in China as a whole.

I would like now to make further reference to the setting up of the communes in 1958 and to the Cultural Revolution in 1966, two landmarks in the progress of the Communist revolutionary tide.

In 1958, Chairman Mao embarked on the greatest and most radical social experiment in the history of mankind, affecting 500 million people, in the communes. Christians were inevitably involved in this unprecedented upheaval. They shared in the early disasters and in the subsequent changing thought. But Christians have evidently seen in this new situtation an opportunity to demonstrate a Christian quality of life, of peace and of joy under all circumstances which has made a deep impression on others. Some Christians have so proved themselves by their devotion to duty that they have been elected as cadres and thus enabled them to exercise an even wider influence. Whatever future witness there is to be in China will have to be geared to these new social structures which are now fully accepted and working with a large measure of success.

The second landmark is the great Proletarian Cultural Revolution. One of its aims was to oppose old thinking, old customs, old habits and old cultures. Thus, religion became a major target, though not the only one. Many high ranking party and government officials came under attack and suffered similar indignities to those which Christians endured. But undoubtedly, the Red Guards struck a mortal blow at organized Christianity. The Church ceased to function as an institution and was driven 100% underground, a thing which has happened elsewhere in the Communist world only in Albania. Meanwhile, Chairman Mao was attempting what, theoretically, the Christian Church had always claimed to do, to produce a new man, the totally selfless man, devoted to the service of his fellowmen. Is not this in itself a possible preparation for a fresh hearing to be given to the Christian Gospel by China's masses? There would seem to be a void and an emptiness of spirit in China. And the spiritual barrenness of Communism may well be the preparation for a new sowing of the Living Seed and the reaping of a rich harvest. One thing is certain. The Church did not die during the Cultural Revolution. More and more house groups met as the Church buildings were closed. With the breakdown of law and order, more people dared to listen to Christian broadcasts with a less fear of detection. Despite the wholesale destruction of Bibles, many were hidden and preserved and are being shared today within groups of 20 or 30 or 40. But they are there. God was thus preparing His Church to receive an influx of young believers in the post-Cultural Revolution years. Is it not true to say there was little left of the old Church after the Cultural Revolution, that the Church today is also almost entirely composed of new converts? How otherwise were these new converts brought to Christ? God, in His Sovereign wisdom moved mightily in China in the postwar period. God knew what the future held and He was working then in the light of what the situation is today, notably among university students, large numbers of whom were soundly converted and filled with the Spirit. God, we believe, according to His promises, has kept and preserved them and refined them in the fires for 25 years. Someone is known to have been recently released from prison where he has maintained a steady faith for as long as 15 years and had been used to lead fellow prisoners to Christ, emerging from prison with the same glowing faith as on the day they took him to prison. This man and many others like him of the older generation are the mature Christians who would be a tower and strength to the young Bible-less converts in the new era that lies ahead. The lessons to be learned from this period of our Church History are these:

First — Christians everywhere must distinguish between social and religious issues. They should loyally support good social reforms. Indeed, they have a duty to take a positive lead in this field, for they will not compromise their first loyalty to Christ. Let me quote Joseph Ton, evangelical Baptist Minister in Rumania, whom I met a few years ago in England. This is what he said — "During my time in England, I was confronted immediately with the view that

Christianity has no place in socialism. Despite this and all the restrictions imposed upon our religious life in Rumania, I claimed in England, in the lectures given in various universities, that this is not true. We have a place in a socialist state. My reasoning was as follows. God is the one who has found the new way and He has placed some of us upon it who live in a socialist society. He has revealed Himself to us and made us His children through the new birth. We have not found Him but He has found us. We have not chosen Him but He has chosen us. Since therefore He chose us from within socialism it means He wants us here. The very fact that evangelical Christianity prospers here in Socialism and the number of believers is increasing fast in spite of opposition, certainly, means that God is at work, at work with exceptional power. On the basis that God is taking the initiative, I would give a decided yes to the question whether we have a place in socialism or not. God has given the Christian his place here and it was God-given and no one can deny it to Him. Besides, if God is the one who has shut the Christian within socialism, it means He has a purpose for him, a mission to the socialist society which He has committed to his charge."

The Divine task of the evangelical Christian living in a socialist country, and that applies to China as well as to Rumania, is to lead such a correct and beautiful life that he will demonstrate and convince the society that *He* is the new man which socialism seeks and desires. Secondly, Christians in countries threatened with a communist takeover must be preparing themselves now by the memorization of Scripture and by cultivating small group fellowship or cell groups, especially within the family and between parents and children. Only in these ways can they be prepared themselves for the possibility of going underground if necessary.

Yes. Our Lord said He would build His Church. This is what He has done already in China in the past. He is still building His Church in China today. Not man's Church. It is His Church and His alone. Man's laboriously built structures have already been swept away but not even hell itself, much less hell's minions can prevail against the Living Church which our risen Lord continues to build in China, not for the glory of any human organization but for His own glory alone.

Chapter 4

The Church in China Today

By Dr. Ted Marr

I have asked many Christians who have left China to share their experiences with you here, but they were all very afraid. Perhaps those sitting here feel that we may have done something wrong, by not inviting one of them to bear witness here. But I would like you all to think deeper: have you ever experienced the things that they have experienced? Their fear is something which we cannot imagine. In collecting the information which I am going to share with you, I have received help from many people. Information has been provided by many concerned Church members in China. Thus, what I am going to talk about is not a thesis, it is a living testimony. I am simply sharing a witness on their behalf.

If we talk about the Church in China today, there are probably two types of Church. One is the "official Church" which we have already read something about. The other type is the "unofficial Church." I am going to talk about the latter. Our Lord Jesus Christ said "Whenever two or three people gather in my name, there am I in the midst." Whenever He is with us, that is the Church. The Church does not necessarily have a beautiful building with rows of seats inside. The Church simply means that our Lord Jesus Christ is there.

In general, the Church in China can be divided into five types. The first is the "personal type," a Christian who simply keeps his faith secret since he does not have the chance to communicate with other Christians. The second type of Church is the "family type." The whole family believe, pray and worship together. The third type is "kinship type," relatives and friends meet together in groups and worship the Lord. The fourth type is a whole group with a commitment to Christ. This type of Church is generally larger, with thirty to forty people of similar commitment. The fifth type is the big gathering of more than several hundred people. We find that these five kinds of Churches have different characteristics in different districts. As Rev. Leslie Lyall mentioned, the information we have been able to gather is only about Central China, Southern China and the coastal areas. Information from North China and the interior is very scarce. May I remind you again that I am only sharing the witnesses of others for them. Some 95% of the information here was given to me personally, so these are personal experiences.

There are four districts we can mention briefly here. The first is Chekiang, Kiangsu, and Central China. The second district is the province of Kwangtung. The third district is Fukien, and the fourth is the North-west. The information we have collected about the North-west is second-hand. Rarely is there first-hand information from there. At the same time, we find that Churches in the cities have a different style from those in the villages. I would like to talk about these three main aspects, that is five different types of Churches, four different districts and two types of life style. In the provinces of Chekiang and Kiangsu we, of course, find that there are individual Christians. In fact, I believe that there are quite a lot of Christians in every district. I have met Christians from all districts telling me that they have never contacted others in them. In Chekiang and Kiangsu we know that "family type" and "kinship type" churches are found, but the major type is the small groups with similar commitment to Christ. Especially in Shanghai, we find that there are quite a lot of family gatherings, where relatives and friends also come along. Sometimes the meeting has thirty to forty people. At other times, it may have around one hundred people. That will be a big gathering but it is not found regularly. In Kwangtung we find that there are only "personal type," "family type" and "kinship type" churches. Small cell groups and big gatherings are comparatively rare, though our information is not very reliable. I remember one very young girl. She is in Hongkong now, but became a Christian in Canton. When we talked to her, I saw that she was very small in size, not over ninety pounds in weight. She told us that she had been even thinner when she decided to come to Hongkong after she had believed in the Lord Jesus Christ. I wondered how such a young girl could survive the experience of swimming the whole night to come to Hongkong.

In the province of Fukien, we thank God that there are not only "family type", "personal type" and "kinship type" churches but that big gatherings are also found. You may have heard already about the great revival in Foochow. The testimony of this has been written down in many places as well. One of the leaders (there are about three of them) who was imprisoned once during the Cultural Revolution, still bears witness for the Lord now. In the North-west, we know that a group of Christians has fellowship in a labor camp. Every morning before work, they have a time of prayer. This is the time and style of their meetings. Besides these, there are quite a lot of wonderful things happening in the villages also. We know that near Canton and NingPo, there are one or two villages which are entirely Christian. The believers stayed there, kept their faith and continued to work. The whole village commune is composed of Christians.

What are their meetings like? They are not easy. Their places of meeting are not fixed, especially for the small cell groups. Our churches outside China have fixed times for meetings, times for morning worship and times for the morning prayer meeting. Their times of meeting are not fixed. Generally speaking, the usual time for meeting is in the afternoon, not in the early morning or at night. We are used to saying that we have our worship on Sunday, but under China's government, only a personal method of individual devotional study can be followed. Every six days there is a holiday, so if all of you have a holiday, or your day of rest falls on the same day, you can have this type of meeting. The meeting place can be changed. Nor is the time fixed. We often say that the Chinese have no sense of time, but being without it is very important here. You must not all arrive at the same time, whereas choosing different times for arrival and leaving will not draw people's attention to it. When all are gathered at one place, there is not usually a fixed program for the meeting.

Hymn-singing, prayer, Bible-exposition, witness and sharing together are the usual pro-gramme. We learn that they are very keen spiritually. Under very difficult circumstances, they still keep their faith. One sister, having joined one of these cell group meetings, told us her experience. In a room about eight feet wide and 16 feet long, thirty to forty people were gathered. The room was very dark with only one light on. The group sang softly and praised the Lord together. Such a cell group is usually held in different districts within a particular city or area, since believers cannot go to the more distant places. Sometimes, there are other places where meetings can be held. God provides quiet mountains, or individuals go out to the country-side and worship God in the early morning. Christians can also eat lunch together in the park and have quiet workship while doing so.

We thank the Lord that churches in China can experience "contextualization." We tend to feel that the Church must always have an identical form, but God's Church can exist under any social system, and it does not need the usual Church Council meeting to decide the form of worship. Many times, if it is a "family type" and "kinship type" meeting, the time of meeting varies arbitrarily, depending on when people are free.

One Chinese told us her story. She is a secondary school student, a young intellectual. She was sent to the countryside after completing her studies. Everytime she came back home from the countryside, she had the opportunity to have fellowship with Christians. Sometimes, they share and meet until very late at night. Generally speaking, the length of the meeting was at least half an hour, and the most usual period seemed to be two hours.

Who are these Christians? From the information that we have collected, we feel that the majority are middle aged, that is those 30-40 years old. They make up over half of all Christians in China. The second group is the old people, occupying about one-third of the total number. Young people constitute the lowest number, those under thirty years old, who make up the remainder. The above does not mean that there are no young people. We have heard of a group in which nearly all are young people. During the great revival in Foochow, we know that many of those saved were young people. Two-thirds are female and one-third male. Among the young people, the ratio between male and female is about equal. Most of the females are in the older age group. We thank our Lord. Perhaps you would ask what they do during the meeting and how they share with one another. One account is taken from a hand-written manuscript which a group of believers used in China. I think we can share two passages from it. Firstly, there is a list of the seven things a believer must do:

1)   Faith must be kept to the end.
2)   Satisfaction in eternal hope must be kept

to the end.

3) The hope from prayer and courage must be kept to the end.

4) God's order must be respected to the end.

5) We must endure to the end.

6) We must trust Jesus loves us to the end.

7) We must believe Jesus saves us to the end.

In addition, there are seven points for everyday:

1) He carries our burden everyday (Ps. 55:22, 68:19, I Pet. 5:7)

2) Proclaim His salvation everyday (Ps. 96:1-2)

3) Praise His name everyday (Ps. 145:1-2)

4) Seek His way everyday (Is. 58:2)

5) Take up His cross and follow Him everyday (Lu. 9:23)

6) Encourage one another everyday (Heb. 3:12-14)

7) Study the Scriptures everyday (Acts 17:10-11)

All Christians face difficulty. We have mentioned singing and Bible reading, but many people may ask whether there are any Bibles and hymn books. My answer is "yes," but they are not as beautiful as our printed ones, they are hand-written only. Christians in China have a few pages of the Bible and a few sheets of hymns. They have hand-written Bibles and printed ones as well. We have interviewed several sisters. They told us that many Christians hid their Bibles during the Cultural Revolution. One sister wrapped her Bible with yellow paper and put it in a hole in the wall and then covered it up with bricks, hoping that she could bring it out for use again one day. We must thank God that we still have contact with brothers and sisters inside. Among all the witnesses whom I have heard, all except one which I know of have listened to the Far East Broadcasting Company's programs. God gives us contact in Christ. Sections of this broadcasting program can help their spiritual life.

I noted at the beginning that the Church in China is not an underground Church in the strictest sense because an underground Church cannot bear witness. It cannot be seen. Let me remind you of a passage in the 1974 "Pray for China Bulletin" describing a public Christian witness at a funeral. We met the sister concerned. She told us that there was a Christian ceremony at the funeral, which was used as a public witness.

Another method of witness is that a lot of young people from Hongkong go to China and have a chance to contact and bear witness to the young people around Canton. Thus, we see that even under the present social system, there is still a witness to God. And how do the young people become converted? God uses periods of upheavals to stir them. Generally speaking, after a youth has finished at his secondary school, he has to face a great mountain, the problem of being sent to the countryside, being moved to a place far away from his home. For nearly all young people, it is a turning point in their emotional lives. Many young Christians whom we have contacted were converted at that time. This was not always the first time they heard the Gospel, because their relatives and friends in some cases had contacted them in previous years and told them about God's truth. It was only at that time that they received Christ as their Saviour. We thank God again, His Church does exist in China. His Church is alive. We must learn from its example. Yet since the Church in China lives in very different circumstances, we must continue to pray for it. In our prayers, we must mention first of all this group of young people. This is vital. The Church does not have freedom. Yet believe that the policy of the People's Republic of China is changing, more so now than ever before. There may be more opportunities in the future to adopt the contextualization method of witness rather than the traditional method. We pray that God will take care of such groups of believers and let them continue to exist. Yet, because of the lack of spiritual resources, lack of opportunity for Bible study groups, the foundations of truth can be shaken quite easily. A Church without the Bible as its foundation will gradually decline, and false teachings will come in. Third, can we expect any

Church growth? Fourth, we must pray for ourselves because the Christians inside China are very concerned about Christians outside. They feel that we live in a materialistic society. They are thus very much concerned with our possible spiritual decline. These are the things they talk about in their conversations with us. I hope that everyone here will really pray for those who have left China recently to live in Hongkong and elsewhere. The problems of adaptation are still considerable for them. If you have the chance to talk with them, you will immediately know that they have grown up under an entirely different culture and society. Sometimes they may appear to be a little preoccupied with themselves, but I feel that we should try our best to pray for them, so that God will give them a more abundant Christian life.

Chapter 5

Father Ladislas Ladany, Dr. Theodore Marr, David Aikman Symposium: The Religious Policy of the People's Republic of China

A CATHOLIC VIEW

By Fr. Ladany

Let us pray. "God, let us see and understand the situation of Christians in China. Not as foreigners see it from abroad. Not even as Chinese see from outside. But as you see it. And let us understand what Christians themselves feel and think inside China. Amen."

I suppose, when you hear of "The Catholic View," it doesn't mean "The Catholic View." There are very few Churches now which are not divided and divided also on the China Christians. I have written a small paper for this conference called "The Church in China: Yesterday, Today and Tomorrow." If you want a copy, drop a line to P.O. Box 13225, Hongkong. Even if you don't put my name there I'll receive it.

I'm supposed to give you I imagine, a brief picture of the history of the Catholic Church in China during the last 25 years. Before I say that I'm the only Catholic speaker, I will mention that this morning, passing by that column in this hall, there was a nail pinned in there and my shirt was torn. So, I went back and bent the nail. The only good deed I did today. But then, I thought, perhaps we can also bend nails which tear apart the garment of Christ.

In the first few years after the Liberation, as we call it, and on up since 1950, I have read *The People's Daily,* which is a kind of daily Bible of Peking. In 1953, I began publishing a weekly, and so I never missed one single issue of *The People's Daily.* I read it well with greatest attention. So, I'm very much used to thinking what Peking thinks about certain things. Thus, I've got a very distorted mind. For the first years the churches in China were left free. They were very much as the first month the churches in Saigon were left free. But in this post-liberation Saigon, the methods, the process, is very similar to what we witnessed in China. But the speed today is much faster. In China, it was slow. Very patient, a sign of great endurance on the part of the Communists. The Communists are not revolutionaries, mind you. They are professional revolutionaries which is a very different thing. It means you have your timetable. You plan your things very carefully and you go step by step. So, the first few years the Church was left free. The first organization tackled in the Catholic Church was what was called the Legion of Mary. In Chinese, it was called *Seng Mu Chin*, which meant Army of Mary. Well, this served. It must be an underground armed organization they reasoned, because the Legion of Mary was a group of youngsters all over the country sent to the hospitals only to preach Christ. Nothing else. Well, then, they had to register and they were in trouble. But the Communists said, "With the Church — we have nothing against it."

Then, came the next step. It was finding that these foreign missionaries were naturally, foreign spies. So, they were arrested one after another. Arrested. You have here one gentleman, probably not only one, but one I know who has spent four years as a guest of Chairman Mao at the expenses of the Chinese government, in prison. Then, these groups, missionaries, some without being arrested, many after a few years in prison — were sent out of China. I don't think any of them were sent out on religious grounds, accused for religious motives. But, of course, that was their motive. It took about five years,

I think, roughly, until practically all were out. I think all were out. Around 1955 or '56, I think that hardly any of them — except an American Bishop, Welsh, who had been arrested and was in prison and maybe a few others — was still there. At the same time began the harassment of the Chinese clergy and faithful.

After the foreigners were out, at the same time, I said, the Chinese were also harassed. I knew a country priest, a very simple man, who was arrested. I really don't know why, but I know from witnesses at his trial, it was a public trial, he made a great witness of his faith. He explained in plain terms what faith meant to him. He was never seen since.

Then there was the matter of 1955. Bishop Kung, the Chinese Bishop of Shanghai, was arrested. And that could cause great stir because he was a kind of national leader of the Church at that time. After he was arrested, most of the Catholics, everybody in China, Catholics or not, were organized in small groups, small discussion teams. They are so even in the present day. Well, the Bishop of Shanghai had been arrested. These small groups had to come together and to express their opinion whether they approved or disapproved of this act of the government. It was still 1955, during the early years. Well, the Catholics tried to keep their consciences clear. Everybody read their local newspaper and they didn't see that Bishop Kung Pi-mei was a great criminal; he was hiding Bibles in his house for this — probably some kind of listing — and that. But, "What is your opinion, your conscience, Mr. Chan?" The Communists would ask. And Chan or Wang would answer: "My opinion is, that the newspaper says that Bishop Kung Pi-mei was a great criminal." "No, no, no. What is *your* opinion? Not what the newspaper says." I heard this story from a personal friend who said, "This was for us, for our consciences, a very painful thing." In these small meetings, small team discussions, you have to express your opinion. And you are not even supposed to say that you are fully in accord because then they'll say you are not sincere. You must say, "I'm hesitating sometimes. But now, I'm trying my best. I understand that the government is right." Bishop Kung to my knowledge is still in prison. Twenty years after I left China we have never had any news that he has died.

In those years, the churches were still open; some churches, as I recall, actually a large number were. Foreigners went in to see them. I remember a certain cabinet minister, a very good Christian. He went in to a church and everyone looked for the priest. He told me after that that they were honest with him in everything about what was wonderful and free in that country. "Religion is perfectly free," he assured me. Still, on each occasion, a representative of the party was present. Once, he went up to the first floor with a single priest who spoke French. Just one floor higher. It happened that as the two descended again, the priest said in French, "Don't believe a word we are telling you." Thus, my friend was enlightened. You see, when many people leave China, be assured that they cannot say what they think. Take the Bishop of Nanking, a very illustrious man, who spoke to Americans alone without a party representative being present. And I knew exactly what he had to say: that the Christians in Nanking don't want to come to Church, that they are enlightened in . . . another direction. I am sure that Bishop Ting in Nanking, speaking to his visitors, knew and understood that he could not say anything else. They didn't know this. Nor did the Christian Press realize that Bishop Ting could only say certain things. This is the situation in China. Very misleading.

Ever since the beginning of the new regime, the Bureau of Religious Affairs, under which Muslims were organized into a unity under the Ministry of Culture, was in charge of all religions. The last religion to submit was the Catholic Church in 1957, when after great difficulties a national conference was held and the National Faculty Catholic Association was established. Even then, it was said that, "We don't want a Rector from the Holy See, from Rome. But you will be an independent established organization under the government."

But actually, when you are under the government, you are under the United Front Department of the Communist Party. And that is so clearly said. Everybody who is not in the party is under that United Front Department of the Party, religions and other entities.

The church existed in a difficult situation. A year after began the consecration of the Nation of New Bishops, without the knowledge of any higher authority, without the knowledge of Rome. During the following four or five years, 45 priests were made Bishops by order of the government. Many churches were closed. But in the major cities, some churches were opened and run by those priests who were ready to sign that they joined this patriotic church. Many refused — went to jail and into forced labor. But there was a group that did sign. And they were not all bad fellows, mind you. Although some of them did not live exactly a Christian life, others were quite exemplary. And they took the office encouraged by others. They saved what could be saved. The desecration lasted roughly until after the Cultural Revolution. The church existed in a very truncated, very paralyzed way. But still, some churches were open.

The Cultural Revolution, as you know, made a grand sweep of all religions. Within two weeks, the Red Guards went into churches, burned Bibles, broke statues and altars . . . the whole thing was finished in seconds. An act of extra-ordinary vandalism. And the churches that survived about nine years later remained closed. We hear from visitors, Chinese or foreign, that some places are used for factories. Coal. I got a picture from a church in Manchuria — the tower was divided into living quarters.

In 1971, an Italian delegation came to Peking and asked to hold a Catholic service. They were told, "Sure," and they started the Sunday Mass in a church in Peking. A few months later, some embassies demanded a Protestant service. They had a Protestant service in Chinese. And that is still going on, I think, up to the present day. But no other church was opened.

So, when foreign delegations visit China — Christian delegations, that is — they go from one city to another saying the same thing — "I want to go to church." I remember a Catholic group, (Argentinians, I think,) they went and asked in Shanghai where the church was and were told, "Sorry, under restoration." So, they went to Peking and proceeded to the church — the only church open in Peking. There, they were met by three or four priests. "How many Christians are here," the foreigners asked. "Oh, 3,000 — maybe 100,000." They went to the next city. "We want to go to the church." Again the answer, "We are very sorry — under repair." They went to Canton. There the Catholic

Church is right in the center of the city. "We want to go to church." Again the answer "We are terribly sorry, but the church is under repair." But, is it . . . could we see it outside?" "We are very sorry, but outside also under repair."

So, what is the situation now? The post-Cultural Revolution China is not the same as it was before. A young generation has grown up. They were then 14, 15 years and writing, "Red Guard — The year of the Revolver." And they were told, "You are the master of the country." They could walk into any office, you see, and arrest the higher party leaders. That was the time, of course, when the whole civilian party organization was wiped out of power by the army — by Lin Piao, who, of course, is no more. These youngsters grew up. And these youngsters have become difficult to discipline. Now these youngsters are not happy there. They are utterly confused. So, many of them came out, risking their lives, swimming to Hongkong. Many of them died in their attempt. That has stopped now because the Hongkong government no longer welcomes them. But when you see them, you see all types of people. There is no uniformity among the youth in China. You meet all kinds. A young fellow came out a few months ago and I met him recently. Inside, he did not know anything about Christianity. But in Hongkong he met a friend who was a

Christian. And he told me, "I want to be a Christian."

On the other hand, you have another, very intelligent, who is amazed that in this backward place of Hongkong, there are university students who believe in Christianity. Such superstition. One youngster said, "Oh, the Catholic Church? That is the most obscure, dangerous organization in the world." I said, "Maybe. How do you know?" He said, "I saw it with my own eyes." "Did you? How did you see it," I said. "I was seven years old. I passed by the cathedral in Canton, and I saw the security officers taking papers out from the Bishop's house — machine guns, revolvers." So, he grew up with that idea. I said, "Did you know — did you see who put the papers there?" Well, of course, when you're seven you don't think that far. Many, of course, are totally ignorant. You say, "What does it mean, CHIONG GIAOW, religion?" Blank. Nothing.

Inside China there are spots. We know of spots where religion is alive. Very rare, I would say. I remember a man working in a factory as a messenger. He was a very good Christian. And he guessed that the other was. Because in some way, you feel it. For you live in an atmosphere where you have to denounce your friends, where hatred is preached instead of brotherhood — universal brotherhood — because to speak of the latter is considered counter-revolutionary. You don't entirely respect the class, only the class method. Therefore, this fellow felt that a Christian was still visible someway. He stands out by some invisible sign. So, he felt that the other man was a Christian but he didn't dare ask. It is a very universal phenomenon.

On the other hand, very recently, I heard fantastic stories from Canton. Some youths are disillusioned. Mind you, the official news coming up also said, "Marxism is passé." But, of course, it is not very bad to say that. But these youths are so disillusioned. What do they do? They go to fortune tellers. Every youngster — everyone who does not believe a thing. Before he comes to Hongkong, he knows it is dangerous, he goes to an old, blind fortune teller. The fortune teller tells him, "the south wind probably very favorable." Well, he means south. Hongkong is the south . . . But now, it is different. Now, the youngsters do the fortune telling. Very fashionable. Not only that — they come together for spiritistic seances. I couldn't believe it, but there are, I think, several — what in Chinese is called FOO LAN. Something moving in sand, or a plate and showing your fate, what will happen to you or they have a small child as a medium who will talk in the name of the deceased. They say, "No. Not every person takes part. Only youngsters — 18, 28." That did shock me, really, or lifted me up. Because it shows a very great yearning among these youngsters, who feel empty inside. Their illusions, their ideas are faded. And they feel empty. And now they come. They have no access to what we would call religion. So, they want to come to the invisible world to find an answer to their questions. They go up there in a mountain near the airport in Canton. And they go up — big masses of youngsters go. Because when they go up, they probably will be lucky in their enterprise. They try to come out or try to do something. So, you find the spiritual renewal in a very distorted way, which really opens up new vistas for us today.

A PROTESTANT VIEW

By Dr. Ted Marr

The topic we are dealing with is really the confrontation of two life views in a particular time and place. The life view of Communism and the life view of Christianity. What is the meaning for us of this in relation to China, where the prevailing governmental view is Communism, whereas our own life view is Christianity?

I would like to take you back a few years, back to the beginning of modern China after the Ch'ing Dynasty fell in 1911. During the 1920's a number of movements grew up, all of which had a tremendous bearing upon what is happening in China today. In 1919, the most significant event of the year was the May 4th movement, a movement of the students which generated anti-foreignism and anti-imperialism. Young people, at that time, were not able to find a solution for their lives. Western democracy had apparently failed in the light of the tragedy of World War I. Traditional Chinese views, following the Confucian tradition, did not provide an answer for young Chinese in the 1920s. Just then, however, the successful story of the October Revolution in Russia burst in upon China's intellectuals. Here was a formula. The Bolshevik Revolution had proven itself to be something that worked. It seemed to be capable, too.

Thus, began the Communist Movement in China. Men such as Li Ta-chao, Ch'en Tu-tsin, were all intellectuals, university professors. They were the kind of people who met Bertrand Russell and Professor Dewey when these men came to China. At the same time, they felt they had to reject traditional religion and Christianity in particular since it happened to be a religion connected with imperialism. Interestingly, Rev. Princeton Hsu has also mentioned to us that it was at that time that the indigenous Chinese Church movement began. This was a crucial moment in Chinese Church history, a crucial moment in the history of China. From this moment on, the central theme of Chinese politics is nationalism.

Personally, I would like to suggest three

ways of looking at China's religious policy: theory, policy, and implementation. Marx and Engels held that if men can control the physical world, then religion is not necessary, is merely a temporary thing, a reaction to uncertainty, to a basic human inability to understand the universe. In Marxian theory, religion is a superstition, whether we mean folk religion or organized religion. If, however, man is able to control the world, then religion in time will disappear, according to Marx and Engels.

This theoretical position is reflected in China's religious policy. The Communist United Front Policy of 1940 reflects it. The Common Program of 1949, article 5 reflects it. Article 88 of the 1954 Constitution reflects it. Finally, the 1975 Constitution reflects this basic theory. The new Chinese Constitution officially permits "freedom of religious belief." Yet it could easily have said: "No one may have freedom of religion," because such a view would be consistent with Marxism. Yet on the whole China's religious policy today reflects the Marxian belief that religion will eventually disappear quite naturally. There is no real sense that extermination of religion is yet a real priority of China's domestic policy.

Now, as to implementation: The Religious Affairs Bureau since 1949 has had a primary goal of organizing national organizations for each religion. The Protestants had their "Three

Self Movement," the Catholics were given the "Patriotic Society," and so on. The effect was to make independent religious activity outside government or party control impossible. The imprisonment of leaders like Wang Ming-tao, Bishop Kung and Watchman Nee, was part of the process of amalgamation and control of religious groups. Significantly, during the Great Leap forward from 1958 to 1960, especially when failure was apparent, religion re-surfaced. It came under intense attack during the Cultural Revolution. More recently, there has apparently been some debate in the Chinese leadership over what attitude should be taken towards religion: a hard or a soft one. Such ambivalence suggests a strong residue of belief in the Marxist axiom that religion will inevitably fade away by itself. I personally believe the holocaust that happened during the Cultural Revolution, when Church buildings were destroyed, and Bibles being taken away, was not part of a systematic extermination of Christianity. It was subservient to a national effort of larger dimensions. It was merely a by-product of something else, just as all the other anti-Christian movements have been.

Now let us examine our own theoretical position. It is very clear: man needs God. In Romans 2, verses 15 and 16, we read: "Which shew the work of the law written in their hearts, their conscience also bearing witness, and their thoughts the meanwhile accusing or else excusing one another; In the day when God shall judge the secrets of men by Jesus Christ according to my Gospel." The secrets of men. There is no way men can get away from God. Therefore, what I am saying here is, on a theoretical level, a contradiction of what Hegel, Marx and Engels and Mao Tse-tung said about men's religious needs. But this contradiction is clearly also a question of implementation, implementation of the command, "Go ye into all the world, and preach the Gospel to every creature." "They are searching and seeking," said Father Ladany of the Chinese young people to whom he had talked. Thus, my attitude as a Protestant to China's religious policy is a bright one.

Finally, I'd like to call your attention to two other points. First, the early Christians were facing a situation not much different from our Chinese brethren in the Mainland today. The early Roman Empire had a state religion, the worship of Caesar. There was a tremendous persecution of Christians. Christianity was not tolerated. Of course, the degree to which Christians were persecuted was perhaps different. Yet there was a similar conflict of world views. Second, I would like to call your attention to the fact that whatever view of life we hold, it will eventually end up as Godless, unless it is a view based on Scriptures. What we are facing here in China is purely and simply a confrontation of life views. The Chinese Communist government implements its religious policy on the basis of a consistent practical application of its own life view. My personal view is that we Christians, in our religious attitude towards China, should implement our own life view; in the light of God's eternal Word and the Hope that we have in Jesus Christ. Christians ought to be not merely as consistent with their beliefs as Communists are to theirs, but more so.

A JOURNALIST'S VIEW

By David Aikman

It's important when you look at the religious policy of Communist China today to keep the whole idea of the policy within a fairly broad prospective. If you try to isolate what is happening to the Christian churches in China from the point of view of treatment by the government, you get a very narrow view of the entire Chinese political situation.

The first thing to realize is that the religious policy of the government of the People's Republic of China is subordinated to a series of other policies which you could describe as being taken up in a pyramid to the ultimate goals of the regime in both domestic policy and in foreign policy. Without becoming too schematic in my scenario of this, I want to say that the People's Republic of China has immediate, medium, and long-range goals.

I'm going to try and describe what its's like to formulate the religious policy of China from the perspective of the Religious Affairs Commission of the People's Republic of China. As many of you know, the Religious Affairs Commission is directly subordinated to the Central Committee of the Chinese Communist Party.

The goals of China in domestic policy and foreign policy are not concealed. Contrary to what a lot of people imagine, there is nothing secret about what China wants, either for herself as far as her present government goes, or for the structure of the world. Let me quote a frequently repeated dictum of Chinese Foreign Minister Ch'iao Kuan-hua: "There is great disorder under heaven. The situation is excellent." Another quotation which you very often find almost in every general speech on China's foreign policy at any international forum, say at the United Nations, is this: nations want independence, countries want liberation, the people want revolution." The people should really have a capital "P" because people is a very specific definition. I do not want to go into that here. But essentially this is the outlook in foreign policy of the Chinese People's Republic within which the religious policy of the Chinese government is elaborated. In domestic policy, obviously, the objectives of the People's Republic of China's government are to create a socialist state within China, to build socialism. Thereafter, at some as yet, and no doubt never-to-be-defined point in the future, China in theory will then make the transition to Communism. Thus, essentially speaking, everything in terms of domestic, social and political policy that would be related to the religious policy of the Chinese People's Republic is to be found within the context of China's foreign policy and domestic policy. Another quotation should make this even clearer. Speaking to a group of Foreign Ministry Officials in March of 1975, (this speech was not published in the outside world but was made available through certain sources) Chiang Ch'ing said: "the goal of our foreign policy is world Communism." Now, I'm not being a cold warrior. I'm not trying to stir up the "fires of reaction," to use a popular Soviet cliché. I'm stating a fact. China's religious policy can only be understood as part of the context for creating in the world conditions which will lead to world Communism internationally, and domestically within China, conditions which will promote first socialism, then Communism domestically, through various economic and social policies.

The medium-term goal to achieve this within China includes a campaign to strengthen even further domestic political control. China is constantly gripped by political struggle of its own devising to eliminate revisionism from its body politic. Domestic political control means power in the hands of those for whom the ultimate goal of Communism is paramount. In foreign policy China acts in pursuit of this as follows: First, to improve existing diplomatic relations and to expand them; second, to isolate the active supporters of the United States and of the Soviet Union, countries which are still allied with the United States or at least sympathetic towards American foreign policy or Soviet foreign policy objectives; and third, actively to assist revolutionary movements, whether by propaganda or by material means in every country — and this is a very important point — in every country where the Communist party is not pro-Soviet. This explains why the Chinese were very careful not to interfere in Portugal, because the Portuguese Communist party is a very pro-Soviet Communist party. Obviously, it's not in the interest of China to see the Portuguese Communist party come to power as long as it supports Moscow.

When we look at the ups and downs of Chinese domestic policy, we can see that from 1949 there have been periods of waxing and waning of radical or revolutionary fervor in government policies. In broad terms, to take an example, 1966 to 1969 was the time of the Great Proletarian Cultural Revolution — a time of tremendous radicalism internally and in foreign policy. Most of the Chinese ambassadors around the world were recalled to Peking. It seemed as if China was, at that time, trying to isolate herself totally from what was going on in the world. During 1969-1971 there was some kind of consolidation process, as the army managed to quell the more anarchic revolutionary trends within the country. And in 1971-1972 there was a definite and noticeable relaxation in all areas of Chinese life, both domestically and internationally. Now, in religious policy, the Chinese government's attitude towards religion in China must be seen as subordinate to the other principal social and political developments of each period of time that we are considering. For example, the religious policy of China during 1966-1969, which somebody else will discuss in detail, is obviously a reflection of the tremendously strong revolutionary currents that were prevailing during the time of the Cultural Revolution. Similarly, the situation domesically in China today will be reflected in today's religious policy. The filtering-down of overriding policy attitudes is what determines national and local treatment of religious believers in China. It is the twists and turns of China's constant political struggle that decide whether any level of religious activity is specifically to be permitted inside China, and that struggle is influenced as much by international developments as by purely arbitrary events in Peking.

Now, you'll notice that I said very little specifically about Christianity. This is for a very specific reason. It's helpful if Christians realize that their religion has not been singled out from sheer vindictiveness for specific attention in China. It is certainly true that at certain periods of time, Christians have been persecuted much more fiercely than other people. The reason for this was not intrinsic to the Christian faith as such, at least, not consciously by Peking, but more to the need for the Chinese government to achieve certain objectives of control.

Religious policy in China is generally implemented through what are known as the mass organizations. As you know, every communist country has basically two forms of control. One is the vertical control through the Communist party, the central committees, the provincial committees, the district committees and so on. The other is through horizontal organizations organized according to profession, class origin, economic group, special interests. For example, religious policy in China regarding the Christian church is part and parcel of domestic policy towards other organizations such as intellectuals, writers, doctors and businessmen. How China treats its Christians can only be understood in the quite broad context. We cannot merely ask "What is the Chinese government doing towards the Christian church at such and such a time?" We cannot, indeed, comprehend what it is doing without enquiring what the Chinese government is doing to other social categories, not necessary religious, at the same time.

It is noticeable that whenever the situation for Christians is slightly easier, it is also slightly easier for Buddhists and for Muslims. For example, during the period of relaxation, beginning in April 1971 with China's thaw towards the U.S., there was evidence that other religions were going to be accorded lighter treatment than they had been during the Cultural Revolution. For example, the Chinese contingent for the annual pilgrimage to Mecca in 1971 was the second largest of all the foreign contingents at Mecca. This was obviously the result of a policy decision by the Chinese government. It wasn't because Chinese Muslims hadn't got around to thinking about going to Mecca until that time. Thus, when we look at treatment of China's Christians as part of Chinese religious policy, it isn't necessarily something specially concocted for Christians. There may be some aspect of the treatment that is peculiar to China's foreign policy.

To sum up, we should be clear in our mind what China's overall domestic and international priorities are before leaping to conclusions about the country's religious policy. Of one thing we may be sure: if China is ideologically at peace with herself, Christians, among others, will be at peace too.

Chapter 6

Marxism, Leninism, The Thoughts of Mao Tse-Tung and Christianity

By David Aikman

"May the words of my mouth and the meditation of our hearts be always acceptable in thy sight, O Lord, our Strength and our Redeemer."

Ephesians 6:12 — "For we wrestle not against flesh and blood, but against principalities, against powers, against the rulers of the darkness of this world, against spiritual wickedness in high places."

Permit me to read to you now, with the indulgence of my excellent interpreters, an item from the Vietnamese News Agency, datelined Hanoi, July 16, 1975. I quote: "It is hard to describe our emotion at the sight of the altar of Uncle Ho in this southernmost part of our homeland. Moving along the Sung Canal, our powerboat took us to a humble-looking temple built on stilts under the big canopy of a mangrove forest. We climbed steps also made of mangrove wood. The first thing we saw in the temple was a portrait of President Ho hung at the center of an altar, flanked by a still new, yellow-starred red flag. The interior was decorated with watercolors of mangrove forests done by an artist who visited the temple some years ago when the enemy still held the area in their grip. The mangrove trees had struck their roots so deep in this alluvial soil of the Mekong Delta that no force could uproot them. Braving rain and storms, the deep-rooted mangrove trees in this village of Vietnam had stood firm and sheltered the altar of Uncle Ho from the prying eyes of the U.S. and its puppets. There was no dust on Uncle Ho's portrait and no mold on the floor, although the altar had no custodian. The altar was the emblem of the local people's undying confidence in the revolution, inspite of their untold hardships and privations."

Permit me to quote from the late Lin Piao — "Once Mao Tse-tung's thought is grasped by the broad masses, it becomes an inexhaustible source of strength and a spiritual atom-bomb of infinite power."

Permit me to quote from Chairman Mao — "We must have faith in the masses and we must have faith in the party. These are two cardinal principles. If we doubt these principles, we shall accomplish nothing. We must have faith first that the peasant masses are ready to advance step by step along the road of socialism under the leadership of the party and second, that the party is capable of leading the peasants along this road." "Not to have a correct political point-of-view is like having no soul." "What kind of spirit is this that makes a foreigner selflessly adapt the cause of the Chinese People's liberation as his own? It is the spirit of internationalism, the spirit of Communism from which every Chinese Communist must learn." "A Communist should have largeness of mind and he should be staunch and active, looking upon the interest of the revolution as his very life and subordinating his personal interests to those of the revolution. He should be more concerned about the party and strengthen the ties between the party and the masses than about any individual, and more concerned about others than himself. Only thus can he be considered as a communist." "The theory of Marx, Engels, Lenin and Stalin is universally applicable. We should not regard it as a dogma but as a guide to action. Studying it is not merely a matter of learning terms and phrases but of learning Marxism-Leninism as the science of revolution." And finally, "We communists are like seeds and the people are like soil. Wherever we go, we must be united with the people, take root, and blossom among them."

That's the end of a series of quotations I wanted to give you. I want you to hold those quotations in your mind as we proceed to look into Marxism-Leninism, the Thoughts of Mao

Tse-tung, and what these mean in relation to our faith. I don't think it is much use trying to prove in a semantic and technical way, that communism is a religion in the narrow sense of the word. If you spend time trying to prove this, you end up wasting more time defining the word religion than you do explaining what Communism is. This is sort of a circular argument which develops and leads nowhere.

I would like to describe Communism as a system of beliefs. I think Christians ought to take far more trouble than they have, to find out what these beliefs are. They are very specific, they are easy to find out. You can get free Communist literature almost anywhere in the world. These beliefs satisfy the emotional and intellectual needs of people. They claim to satisfy the spiritual needs of people. But, of course, they do not admit that there are spiritual needs. When I speak of Communism in China, I do not mean the system of political control by the Communist Party with all the well-known restrictions upon freedom of worship, freedom of activity. I mean a system of beliefs, an ideology as the Chinese themselves call it, which goes by the name Marxism-Leninism, Mao Tse-tung Thought.

I am going to refer to some theoretical things. I have a very sound reason for wanting to talk about this. We are often inclined to say that theory does you no good, you need experience and you need practice. But those of you who have taught young men going out in the ministry, and young women going to be missionaries, would you let such a person preach if he hadn't been taught the Word of God, if he did not know the Bible? Would you let him preach? Why would you not let him preach? Because you believe the Bible is the Word of God. Marxism-Leninism, Mao Tse-tung Thoughts is the "word" of Communism in China.

There is another reason why we should study theory apart from the intrinsic, common-sense reason for doing so. Communists in China believe that theory is an absolutely indispensable basis for action. Communists believe that you cannot make the right action in political, social, economic and historical terms unless you have the right theory. Chairman Mao himself says, "The theoretical basis guiding our thinking is Marxism and Leninism."

Chairman Mao Tse-tung has also stated: "Communism is at once a complete system of proletarian ideology and a new social system. It is different from any other ideological and social system and it is the most complete, progressive, revolutionary and rational system in human history." These are the claims made on behalf of theory by those who attempt to practice it.

In China, recently, there was a campaign going on trying to teach people about the importance of the dictatorship of the proletariat. Those of us who try to understand China from the outside often shake our heads and say, "Why do they spend so much time concentrating on dry theory. Don't they realize that these people are not stupid?" Yes. They realize that, but they also realize something else. If you don't continually justify forceful actions by relation and reference to some kind of absolute, you're very quickly going to lose whatever legitimacy you had for making those forceful actions. We know this as Christians. We know that we cannot go out and preach the Word of God unless we believe that's what Christ taught us to do. If it were optional, why should we worry about it, why should we bother? Why would there be anything such as a missionary school or a Bible college?

Now, there are two essential aspects to the belief system of Communism, or, to spell it out again, the belief system of Marxism-Leninism and the Thought of Mao Tse-tung. One aspect is essentially intellectual. It makes a certain intellectual play. It puts forward certain theories which it says are the basis for everything else. Another aspect, and to my mind there's not the slightest doubt about it, is essentially spiritual. You can understand Communism perfectly in an intellectual sense and you might never understand why a man will give up his entire life to sacrifice his personal interest for the revolution. Take the Portuguese Communist Party. Tortured, beaten, starved, driven underground. Those men, for 30 or 40 years, have struggled to build up a machinery of political control. And recently, it seemed as if the whole of Portugal was within their grasp. A handful of people. A handful of people. They didn't have God on their side, but did pretty well, through the sheer, forceful human attributes of self sacrifice. Let's get to the intellectual aspect of Marxism and try to see roughly what we're dealing with, so that we can then move on to the spiritual aspect, and understand it a little bit better as Christians.

I have studied Marxism-Leninism and Mao Tse-tung Thought for a number of years. There's a sort of fascination about it which at times, one must admit, is dangerous. It's like studying poisonous spiders. They're very beautiful but they're deadly. I'm convinced, and I make this premise straightout, that Communist belief, and I emphasize the word belief, is a specifically diabolical parody of the Christian faith specifically, in exactly the same way that homosexuality is a diabolical parody of the perfect relationship between man and woman. It's a parody of Christ's relationship to His Church. It's a parody of God's relationship to Israel. The devil cannot create. He can only imitate. But he copies very well. Let's see how.

When you start reading Marx, or when you start reading about Marxism before you get on to Lenin or anything else, you find that there is a tremendously strong drive to arrive somewhere intellectually. If you are fairly sensitive, you realize that he is doing more than simply trying to solve an intellectual problem. Marx desperately needed, for his own satisfaction of mind, to prove to himself that there was no God, that the universe was under the control of abstract laws, and yet, at the same time, that there could be salvation for man. At the heart of Marx's thinking is a desire to wipe out, in his own heart, I think you have to get down to that, the idea of God, and at the same time to provide hope for himself, and therefore, since there is no such thing as man identified solely with God, salvation for the whole human race.

When you look at Marxism, you find that step by step, the building up of the theory of Marxism is a systematic denial of the Christian concept of God, of creation, of faith, of redemption, of sin, of righteousness, of everything that is fundamental to Christian belief. There is a systematic denial. And the attempt to wipe out any vestige of Christian belief or Christian theory, if you like, was carried on by Engels, and then by Lenin, and then by Stalin and then by Mao. And do you know what happened? Mao, in his desire to answer certain personal, intellectual and moral needs of his own, he too sought salvation. He, too, wanted hope for the human race. And he, too, didn't want the idea of a personal God. But Mao ends up categorically denying in his statements a very large number of the basic principles of Marx. You wouldn't think so, but you are going to see, when I give you a few quotations.

The most frequently quoted quotation of Karl Marx is, "Philosophers have merely interpreted the world in different ways. Our purpose is to change it." Marx, however, did set out to explain the world as he saw it. He had to explain it in a way which was internally consistent with everything that one could see in the visible world, and everything that was then known about the nature of the human beings and the nature of human society. And Marx quickly found that you cannot explain the world satisfactorily without God unless you create a new absolute. Something which is final, definite, you could say that the absolute for Marx, the final reference point, is history. In a way, another word for it would be nature. I'm not going to go into Hegel and dialectics. And I'm not going to go in any detail into Marx's theory. But I do want you to have the very basics in your mind as we look at Marxism intellectually to proceed through to Mao intellectually, in order for us to understand better the whole spiritual point of what we're studying this morning.

The dialectic of history, according to Marx,

is the explanation of, and these are not his words, "Why the world is in a mess." Marx had to explain why people exploited each other, why there were wars, why people weren't happy. From the beginning, he ruled out any kind of moral values as an explanation for this. He had to do that. If he had allowed in any moral values, they would have led him inevitably to God. Marx was an honest man intellectually. He genuinely sought a truth but he didn't want to find God. So, he had to find a way of an absolute without God. And the only way he could do that was to deny morality completely. Communists sometimes accuse Christians and Westerners and non-Communists of every nationality of distorting Marx. That's not true. We have Marx's own words. Marx himself said about morality, "The Communists do not advocate selfishness as against devotion or devotion as against selfishness. Nor do they speak against this theoretically in its simple form or in its ideological form. Rather, they show the material origin of morality with which morality will disappear of itself. In short, said Marx, "the communists do not teach morality." According to Marx, history has evolved in a class struggle involving basic competition for the means of production. Marx thought that there were five different stages of human development: the communal system, where everything was held supposedly in agreement, in common, the slave system, the feudal system, the capitalist system and the socialist system. Marx postulated in his theory, that the whole human race was evolving socially and politically towards the ultimate development, Communism, in which there would be no more struggle, there would be no more struggle because there would be no more classes. There would be a classless society. It is in effect a Utopia. But Marx carefully never defined it. Moreover, he spent a great deal of his time attacking people he regarded as Utopian.

Having set-up his theory, which was at once a theory of the nature of the world, a theory of the nature of man, a theory of the nature of economics, Marx sat about trying to implement it. Marx was not just an egghead who sat in a room in London writing with a squeaky pen. He was a revolutionary. He spent hour after hour, trying to organize revolutionary uprisings in Europe. The Communist Manifesto was written in 1848. That was the year of revolutions in Europe, when old societies were being over-turned. But while Marx was a revolutionary, he was not an organizer and he was not a leader of men. If Marx had died, even if Marx had died and Engels had still lived and carried on his work, it is quite possible that Marxist belief would have died out as one of those peculiar varieties of 19th century Philosophical Thought. It is quite possible that we would have never heard today of a Communist Party. But somebody else sprang up, of such incredible human drive, incredible intelligence, and one has to say, almost diabolical knowledge and timing and skill, who not only carried on the message of Marx, but founded it in a state which became the basis of the Marxist crusade to the rest of the world. That man was Lenin.

I defy any Christian who is really filled with the Spirit of God, who is close to the Lord, to read ten pages of Lenin without getting a severe headache. And that's not because it's bad. It's because it's filled with hatred. Lenin wrote volume after volume. A very great deal of it is filled with hatred, hatred of opponents, of any-body who blocked his goal to achieve Communism in the world, by first achieving a revolution in Russia. Lenin was a brilliant man, a ruthless man, a great leader, a man of simple taste, a very attractive personality. He was like an efficient businessman. I don't want to malign the business community — please don't get that idea — but, he is like that type that many of us have met, a businessman who seems to have it all under control, who has clean fingernails, who knows where he is going, who doesn't take any nonsense from subordinates, who is polite and charming — and going to Hell.

Lenin had to develop two new stages of Marxist belief in order to get anywhere with Marxism, and in order to achieve revolution in Russia. First of all, he had to explain how you could have a revolution in a country which was predominantly peasant. After all, the whole point of Marxism is that it's the industrialized proletariat that rises up in the final stage of human development, in the final stage of class struggle, overthrows Capitalism, and leads mankind on into socialism and then Communism. This was orthodox Marxist theory. Lenin, by a misfortune of history one might say, happened to be a Russian and Russia was not an industrialized society. So, Lenin had to rely upon other methods than theory to develop a system of revolution. Lenin developed, and not purely on his own, but with the help of previous thinkers, a whole doctrine of revolutionary action, a doctrine of strategy, a doctrine of tactics. Most important of all, Lenin developed the idea of the party as a priesthood. Lenin would never have used the word priesthood. But there is no doubt at all that the concept of the party that Lenin had, without which Communism can never come to power in any country in the world, is the idea of the priesthood. The party according to Marx is the vanguard of the proletariat. The party leads the working class. The party can never make a mistake. Why not? Isn't the party composed of human beings, non-Communists will say and human beings surely can make mistakes? Yes, says the communist, but you see, Communists have history on their side. Therefore, if it is in the vanguard of history, collectively the party, representing the impersonal working out of the great scheme of human development towards Communism, can never make a mistake. Individuals might be leftist or rightist deviationists, or they might be opportunists, or revisionists, or splitists or revanchists, but the Party with a capital "P" can never make a mistake.

Lenin said of religion, "All religion is utterly vile, utterly horrible." For Lenin, any moral concept which cut across his idea of revolution was intrinsically wrong. The only morality which counted for Lenin, and I am not maligning Lenin, if he were standing here today, he would agree with me, the only morality that counted was revolutionary morality. And what is revolutionary morality? It is the morality of bringing about the revolution in the most efficient way possible. Lenin didn't say so. But he did act it. In this way. If it was necessary to tell a lie for the sake of the revolution, you told a lie. If it was necessary to kill, you killed. You did not worry about it, because the highest goal of all is the revolution. Everything is dedicated to the revolution.

Lenin died in 1924, of an illness brought on after somebody had tried to assassinate him. Mao, just about the time that Lenin died, was beginning to see the scope of what was wrong socially and politically in China. Mao Tse-tung came from a fairly affluent peasant background.

People are found of saying Mao was a peasant, as if this makes him peculiarly foolish and rather uncivilized or something like that. But Mao was a very intelligent man. Mao had the equivalent in an American university of a BA and MA degree. He formally studied the Chinese classics and Chinese literature until he was about 25 or 26. Mao didn't finish his education at the age of 14. Mao was better read in the great writers of western rationalism of the 18th century — men like Montesquieu, Diderot, Voltaire—than are most of those gathered for this conference. He knew more about western thinkers, I would venture to suggest, probably than any western missionary in China at that time.

Mao was concerned from the very beginning with two things: how to change China, to make it strong in the phase of foreign imperialism and foreign oppression; and how to save man. Mao wasn't quite sure, to begin with, whether he should dedicate his life to understanding how to save man or whether he should attempt to save China first. I'm not really being facetious. If you study Mao's earliest writings in 1918 and 1919, you find a tremendous individualistic idealism. Mao was a sort of person who would have taken a Dale Carnegie Course at the first opportunity. Mao would have signed up to self improvement in anything. He was constantly going on long walks in the hills, washing

111

in cold water, strengthening his body. There was a time when Mao believed that physical education would, in fact, solve China's problems. Mao was concerned with human values. He was concerned, in the same way that Marx was, with injustice. But there is an interesting difference. As soon as Marx had began to realize that he was interested in things like justice, and as soon as he began to realize that it would lead him eventually to God, because Marx's parents were Jews who were converted to the Christian faith, Marx went the other way and took no more interest in morality.

But Mao in the 1920's didn't know enough about Marxism to realize that it was unfashionable to talk about morality. Mao read deeply in western writers on morality. He read deeply in Chinese philosophers, for example Wang Fu-chih the Hunanese philosopher who believed that human nature was infinitely perfectable. Mao was tremendously influenced by this thinker. Mao in the Changsha First Normal School, which was where he studied the equivalent of the BA and MA degrees, joined with like-minded people who wanted to make human beings better. But in the 1920's, a Chinese with that kind of interest really only had three or four choices to make. He became a revolutionary, he went abroad, he joined the Kuomintang or he became a Christian. Mao didn't join the Kuomintang officially, although as you will know, there was an alliance between the Nationalist Party, the Kuomintang and the Communists from 1923 until 1927. What Mao did was concern himself with what was happening in the countryside, stirring up revolution, trying to make things better, trying to change the lot of the Chinese peasant. Mao eventually became a very successful peasant leader and an organizer. Gradually, he began to realize that no matter how much he was concerned with morality, with individual situations, nevertheless, he might have said to himself, "The only doctrine that justifies what I am doing is Marxism-Leninism." Mao, rather late in the day, one might say, joined the Communist Party in China. That was in 1921. By 1927 he had begun to make a name for himself. In fact, not a very good name at first. He was severely censured by the Central Committee of the Chinese Communist Party for making mistakes. Nevertheless, in the 1920s, and then, during the 1930s Mao began to read Marx and Lenin and Engels and Stalin, and began to build up a basis of theory to justify the way he thought necessary to change China, to throw out the foreigners and to bring about an improvement in the human being.

Let's stop with Mao at that point and go back to Marx. I said at the beginning that at its heart, Marxism-Leninism, Mao Tse-tung Thought is a diabolical parody of the Christian faith. Let's look at some of the ways in which it does that.

Against the basic concept of God creating the world is set the idea of materialism. There is no deity, there is only a system of laws, impersonal, inhuman, natural laws which affect the way human beings behave. There's no such thing as sin. If you see that things are wrong with the world, that is because the laws of the dialectic, the laws of history, the laws of materialism are being worked out. The idea of salvation is denied in a personal sense, but is affirmed and parodied in the working out of history. How does it happen? Man will be an assistant to history and will save himself. As soon as he learns the news of history, as soon as he reads Marx, studies Lenin, then he will know how to grasp his own personal salvation. The idea of God being in control of the world is completely denied. The liberation of man is in man's hands. Faith is completely denied by Marx. Marx says, "Faith and specially faith in a sacred soul of a community is the last thing that is needed for the attainment of Communism." Remember that, because it is completely contradicted by the quotation we read at the beginning, when Mao was heard to say, "We need faith." We see that the denial of the basic Christian message is carried through in a system of theory and in a system of practice. We talked about revolution and morality. This, of course, is a complete denial of emotion, of absolute

114

morality given by God. But one thing is very peculiar about the development of Marxism and Leninism, and that is that the more the Marxists have tried to suppress Christian thinking and Christian beliefs, the more these ideas have kept popping up again. Lenin, by creating a Soviet state, and by trying to make an institution of all the ideas of Marx, thought that once and for all he had wiped out the idea of God. He thought that religion, that morality as issues in themselves would play no more role in politics and in the development of the world.

As soon as Lenin died, however, the entire concept of the sacred came bouncing back again. We find that a shrine is created over Lenin's tomb. Lenin becomes a saint, and in the manner of old Russian saints, he is embalmed as if he were immortal. Pilgrims queue up for hour after hour to see this saint in a tomb in Red Square in Moscow. Slogans are written up in the streets "Lenin Lived, Lenin lives, Lenin will live," although he has been dead years and years and years. There's a new vocabulary that crops up, exhortations like, "You must protect the sacred soil of our country." "Our sacred duty is to do such and such." We read about Ho Chi Min's altar, a center of worship, not a speck of dust upon it. But then, an even more peculiar thing happens with Mao Tse-tung. Mao, had got to the point where he realized you've got to have faith in an impossible situation or else you can never lead a Communist party in a historical and social setting like China as it was in the 1920s and 30s. Did Mao have faith in Communist theory? Not so much. But he did have faith that something was right about what he was doing, that the peasants would respond to the message. So he changed it around slightly and said, "We must have faith in the masses." But even that was not enough. Mao found himself compelled, because of the nature of Chinese society, because of the nature of the Confucian tradition, because of the Chinese interest in morality, because the Chinese have always said, "It is not laws that change society but people. You do not need good laws, you need good people," compelled more and more toward a concept of personal salvation within Communism.

We have already gone a long way from the Marxist idea of materialism and the unraveling of history and Lenin, from the idea of the party which is a prophetic vanguard of history, the idea of the party as the voice of history in the same way that the prophets in the Old Testament were the voice of God. We've gone a long way from that. When we come to Mao, we find him concerned with what individual peasants think and feel. We've all heard the word "brainwashing." Now this is a genuine expression. It wasn't invented by the C.I.A. Brainwashing refers to a process of changing a person's thinking not simply by argument, not simply by saying, "these ideas are more rational, more intelligent, better for the world than yours," but by conversion. The whole point of re-education in China in the 1950's, and one must assume this is still going on today, is not to torture people into saying, "I believe Mao is the leader of the Communist party, he cannot make mistakes," but to drive people by psychological pressure to the point where they cannot resist the embracing arms of the party which says "Come to us, you have committed sins against the people. But if you come to us, if you realize your mistakes, we will love you and you will be forgiven."

Throughout re-education in China during the 1950s, again and again, and we know this from Chinese who went through it and from foreigners who went through it, there is the idea of sin. It is sin against the people of China because a person was perhaps associated with the Imperialists. There is the idea of repentance. Is a person sincerely sorry for what he has done against the Chinese people? There is the idea of changing one's nature, of conversion. There is the idea of forgiveness. If a person changes his ideas, repents of his sins, then

117

he will be forgiven by the people. And there's not the slightest doubt that this is a parody of the whole basis of the Christian notion of being born again. It's a parody because Mao found out something that Lenin had overlooked and Marx had overlooked. Mao found out that people need to be loved, they need to be forgiven. There is no more valid proof in my mind of the existence of God and of the whole basic Christian message than this, that all the systems that have tried to overthrow Christianity or that have been set-up by Satan to oppose it have ended up copying all its basic concepts. In the Thoughts of Mao Tse-tung, which is what we're concerned about now, we've come back far away from the materialist conception of history, right back to the individual's own personal salvation, until we reach a ridiculous point in the Thoughts of Mao Tse-tung where you can change your class nature by attitude. It no longer matters which class you were born into. If you have the right attitude, you can become a proletariat. Isn't that strange? Salvation to the Jews was owed to them first because they were God's chosen people. God had chosen them. There was nothing they could do about it. They had a right, a birth-right to be God's children. But with the New Covenant, we come to a new situation where a person has that birthright to be God's child, not because he was born into a certain situation, a certain class, but because he changes his attitude towards God. He believes on Jesus Christ and accepts God's forgiveness in a unique personal way.

When I was in Peking in 1972, I talked to the interpreter who had been present when Chairman Mao met Edgar Snow. Chairman Mao, as many of you know, gave several interviews to Edgar Snow in the 1930s, out of which came a famous book, *Red Star over China*. And *Red Star over China* probably did more to influence American thinking in favor of what was going on in the Chinese Communist areas of China than any other single book. I personally believe that Snow was not a Communist or a Marxist. I think he was a sincere man who may at times have been naive, but I believe he reported what he genuinely saw or thought he saw. But on one occasion, when Chairman Mao was being interviewed by Edgar Snow, Mao referred to his own death and used the expression, "When I go to meet God." And I asked Yao Wei, this very fine interpreter who had been present, what expression in Chinese Mao had used? And Yao Wei said, "Chien Shang Ti" which means "to meet God." And I said, "Is that a traditional Chinese expression?" because I knew it wasn't but I pretended to be naive. And he said, "No." So, I said, "What is it?" He said, "It's a

Christian expression." I asked why Chairman
Mao was using a Christian expression. "Oh,"
he said, "anybody who is an intellectual in
China would have used that kind of expression."
Would they?

Let's move to the spiritual aspect. Jesus
says, "Ye shall know them by their fruits."
What are the fruits of the Spirit in Galatians?
Love, Joy, Peace, Patience, Goodness, Kindness,
Faithfulness, Gentleness, Self-Control. "By
this shall all men know that ye are my disciples,
if ye have love one for another." If we do not
love one another, we cannot expect people
to be very impressed by what we say about
Christ. When we look at Marxism-Leninism,
the Thoughts of Mao Tse-tung, we find an
extraordinary thing happening. You take the
fruits of the Christian Spirit and you find
that they are converted into their opposites.
The qualities that are regarded as desirable in
a moral sense, if you like, the moral fruits of
the beliefs in Marxism Leninism, the Thoughts
of Mao Tse-tung, are the opposite of the Christian
fruits of the Spirit. Instead of love, you have
class hatred. You must hate people of a different
class. You mustn't love them. If you love them,
you will hold up history. You will prevent
history from being unraveled. You must not
have joy. You must be angry at exploitation
and things like that. You must not talk about
peace for you must make war. You must be

prepared for war. Mao Tse-tung says a great deal about war. One of the things he said was, "If we are continually afraid of war, we will not be prepared for it when it comes, as it certainly must come." The Chinese government definitely believes that there will be a third world war. Definitely. It is part almost of an article of faith of China's foreign policy. You must not have patience. You must immediately demand higher wages, the overthrow of the government, the acceptance of the demands of this or that revolutionary or terrorist movement. Immediately. Not patience. You must not be good and kind to your enemies. Class enemies must be dealt with mercilessly. No mercy for class enemies. Faithfulness. Was Lin Piao faithful to Mao? Was Mao faithful to Liu Shao Chi? Was Stalin faithful to Trotsky? And so it goes on. Gentleness. I was in Vientiane, Laos in May 1975. As you may recall, the United States Aid Compound had been occupied by Laotian students. Most of these students were not actually Communists. Many of them were sympathetic towards what they understood to be some of the Communist Pathet Lao goals for Laos. Many of them were idealists. If you had been in Laos at that time, you would have recognized in these students the sons and daughters of middle class Americans or middle class Chinese or middle class

Filipinos who were out in the streets in the 1960s. The same people. And they occupied this compound. Because they did so hundreds of people went without money to support their families. And many Laotian USAID workers saw their families almost starve. Negotiations went on between the United States Embassy and the Laotian Government for many days, but nothing happened. Finally, in exasperation, some of the workers in this United States Aid Compound who had been unable to work because it was occupied by the students, marched upon the Prime Minister's office. The delegation of about 500, I suppose, was well-mannered, good humored and they were not going to throw eggs. They were very careful not to identify themselves with the Americans. They didn't want American reporters being visible there, they didn't want to overthrow the Pathet Lao, they didn't want to support the Laotian rightists. They wanted food for their families. They wanted the Prime Minister of Laos to say to the students, "Well, you've made your point. The Americans have signed the piece of paper abolishing this Aid Program. Now, please, will you leave?" That's what they wanted the Prime Minister to do. A delegation of three of these students was led from the place where all of them had been stopped into the Prime Minister's house. They were led in by a soldier of the Vientians, that is to say, the non-Communist side, and courteously received for about 10 minutes. They were watched by a delegation of Pathet Lao Communist soldiers. The delegation of three went back to the group and expalined what it was that the Prime Minister had just told them. They had not been speaking more than about 40 seconds when one of the most ugly incidents I've ever seen in my life occurred. Contorted with rage, shouting at the top of his voice, a huge Communist soldier came up with pistol drawn and told him to stop. The student said, "But I am just telling them what the Prime Minister told us." The Communist soldier said, "You are not allowed to tell people here whatever you think. This is a new situation now." I have never seen a man so angry, so enraged. There was no gentleness at all at that time in that man. And there was no self control.

"The Communists," as Brother Andrew said the first night, "are trying to turn the world upside down, but Christians are trying to turn the world upside up." No purely political system will ever be successful against Communism. Most diplomats of Western countries now, I say this having spoken to many of them, and I make a very categorical statement, most diplomats are incapable of understanding Communist thinking because they themselves have no set beliefs and they do not know what it is like to have a series of set beliefs. We should not oppose Communism in China or anywhere else with democracy. We cannot meet it with political participation, with the Jaycees, with the Parent-Teacher Associations. It is far too late to try anything like that. We should not even waste time on tinkering solutions like that.

"For we wrestle not with flesh and blood." And as Paul again said in Romans — Romans 1 Verse 16 — "For I am not ashamed of the Gospel of Christ. For it is the power of God unto salvation to everyone that believeth" — to the Jew first and also to the Greek, to the person in the non-Communist world first who can still hear freely about the Gospel but also to the man in the Communist world who has never heard about it but will benefit by doing so, and finally — Ephesians again, Chapter 6, continuing on from where we began this talk this morning, "Wherefore," Ephesians 6:13 — "Wherefore take unto you the whole armour of God that ye may be able to withstand in the evil day and having done all to stand. Stand therefore having your loins girded about with truth and having on the breastplate of righteousness and your feet shod with the preparation of the Gospel of Peace. Above all, taking the shield of faith wherewith ye shall be able to quench all the fiery darts of the wicked and take the helmet of salvation and the sword of the spirit which is the Word of God, praying always with all prayer and supplication in the spirit and watching there unto with perseverance and supplication for all saints."

Can we do that?

China's children are its most important resource.

Above: Party rhetoric and visual aids join reading, writing and arithmatic instructions.

Below: China is revising its policy on education to "wipe out the influence of the Gang of Four"

Above: Brother Andrew stops to visit with children living in a housing complex.

Below: Members of the People's Liberation Army are found throughout China.

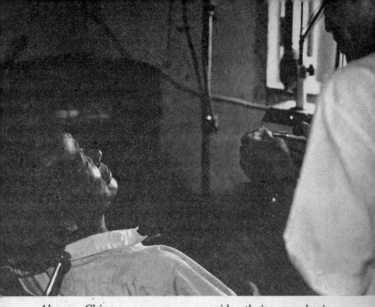

Above: Chinese communes provide their own basic medical and dental facilities.

Below: The arts in China have been used to reinforce government policies.

DABAI HONG HUA BIAN DI KAI!

Above: Mammoth billboards just one of many media means used by the government.

Below: Mourners march through T'ien An Men Square to pay their final respects to Chou En-lai.

Above: Chinese medicine includes the use of herbal drugs.

Below: China's doorway to Asia and much of the world is over this bridge which leads to Hong Kong.

Closed church buildings remain as reminders of earlier days of Christian witness.

Chapter 7
Literature

By Mr. David Wang

I would like to begin my report with two paradoxes. China is a very big country. Therefore, a wise old China watcher once said, "Anything you say about China is true, somewhere. Anything you say about China is false, somewhere." Anyone who says that he understands today's China, is either a fool or a liar. And so I have come to this conclusion as we study China, that it is quite impossible, almost hopeless for our limited minds to try to formulate one single co-ordinated, unified, universally agreeable strategy to reach China for Christ. But praise God, He has a strategy. He always does. Sometimes His strategies may seem funny to us. For example: walking around the walls of the city of Jericho seven times, and then shouting! But that was His strategy, and it worked. Sometimes His strategy seems to be illogical, unreasonable to us. For example: cutting down the army of Gideon to a mere 300 men! But that was God's strategy, and it worked. I have read in the Word of God, as prophesied and stated by the prophet Isaiah, about the sovereignty of God. We read, in Isaiah 40:12-14, "Who hath measured the waters in the hollow of his hand, and meted out heaven with a span and comprehended the dust of the earth in a measure, and weighed the mountains in scales, and the hills in a balance? Who hath directed the Spirit of the Lord, or being His counsellor hath taught him? With whom took he counsel, and who instructed him, and taught him in the path of judgement, and taught him knowledge, and shewed to him the way of understanding?" Nobody, nobody! Our God is a sovereign God, and our God has His strategy, and it is vital that we find out His strategy, that we follow His plan. Any man-originated, program-oriented, computerized methodology may very well fall flat on its face and it deserves to fall flat. Remember that for 150 years we imposed our strategy, we practiced our plans on China evangelization. And what was the result? A generally weak, fragmented, depressed Church. In the mind of an ordinary Chinese today that church was a product of man-centered imperialism and colonialism. Oh, may God help us to learn that it is not by might, that it is not by power, that it is not even by co-ordinated strategies, but by His Spirit and His Spirit alone that any long-lasting spiritual accomplishment can be made for His Kingdom's sake.

And what is God's strategy in these last days? The prophet Joel says, in chapter two, speaking of the Lord: "And it shall come to pass afterward, that I will pour out my spirit upon all flesh." Now, pay attention to this. God will pour His spirit on all flesh, not on all the churches. There is a distinct difference between the Church and the flesh. When God says he is going to pour His spirit upon all flesh I do not believe he merely means the Charismatic movement of today. That is only a part of it. "All flesh" means the unredeemed men and women of our times. And which country has more flesh than today's China? I believe God's strategy is to pour out His spirit upon that land. And what is the purpose of God's strategy? Verse 32 of the second chapter of Joel: "That whosoever shall call on the name of our Lord, shall be delivered." The purpose of God's strategy is that 900 million of our beloved Chinese may call upon God's name and be saved.

God is at work inside China, and has always been during the past 25 years, accomplishing His sovereign purposes, executing His divine strategy. The Bamboo Curtain has always been vertical between human beings, but it has no roof to it. It has never shut God out. The Holy Spirit has had complete and total access to His church inside China during the past 25 years, in executing the divine strategy of God. We may not have been able to execute our missionary strategies, but the Holy Spirit, during the past 25 years, has been executing God's strategy, purifying the church inside China, strengthening Christ's Body inside China, purging and protecting, preserving, helping Christians to take root downward in order to bear fruit upward. God has been executing His strategy. Our strategy therefore as we try to formulate, as we try to work out a strategy for reaching China for Christ, must be parallel to God's strategy. God's program is always right on time. God's program is always perfect. No force on earth or in heaven can derail or detour God's planned route and God's planned schedule.

Therefore I firmly believe that in our China literature program, rather than planning our strategy we should be praying for His strategy. Second, I believe we must consult as closely as possible with the Church inside China today, to discover what their real needs are. Let us give them what they need, rather than what we think they need. In our literature production for our brothers and our sisters inside China a few tests are absolutely essential. With God's help, let us go back and sit at the feet of the Christians inside China and humbly and sincerely ask, "What can we do? Can we be of service to you? What do you need?" and give them, with God's help, what they need. May we guard against returning to the old policy of imposing what we

think is right, of imposing what we think is
needed for the church inside China today. The
same is true in our efforts to reach non-
Christians inside China. I believe, and I strongly
recommend that any evangelistic guidelines to
reach China must be set and decided upon with,
and preferably by, the Christians inside China
today. They have gone through the tribulation.
They have gone through the suffering. They
have not only survived, but have striven for the
glory of God, so let us learn from them how to.
May I make the following concrete suggestions
to the esteemed groups and individuals who are
burdened to prepare literature to reach China
with the life-changing Gospel of Jesus Christ. I
humbly plead, let us get together, regularly,
maybe four or five times a year. Let us get
together to pray, to fast together, to wait upon
Him together, to share, and, if necessary, let us
correct one another in love. Instead of coming
together and patting each other on the shoulder
and saying nice wishy-washy things, like "Bless
you" and "How is your wife" and "How is the
work in Manila," let us say, "Brother, in love,
may I share with you something which the Holy
Spirit has laid upon my heart?" I long honestly,
sincerely, I long for someone to come to me and
say, "Brother David, in love, I want to tell you
something." And my prayer is the prayer of
King David, "Let the righteous smite me; it shall
be a kindness; and let him reprove me; it shall be

an excellent oil, which shall not break my head." Ps. 141:5.

Second, let us seek to develop a specialization system to eliminate duplication and competition. By this I mean, let all of us come together, submit ourselves to the Holy Spirit, submit ourselves to one another, and together chart out the steps. Certain groups should concentrate on producing pre-evangelistic literature while others should concentrate on preparing Scriptures for China or on Christian maturity and leadership and so on. Thus we will not be duplicating or fighting with one another. Rather, in a practical way we can work with one another as co-laborers with the Lord.

Third, let us together publish and up-date a resource catalogue regularly informing Christians who have a burden for China what specific literature is available now, what is in the planning stage, and what is in the preparation stage and from what source or sources this literature is available. Thus people can come to Christian groups for certain types of literature that they might, with God's help, bring to their relatives inside China. Or they may use this literature to reach Chinese who come out from China. By no means am I suggesting that we form an intricate system of committees and sub-committees, chairman and vice-chairmen, I am not suggesting that. That only complicates, rather than implements. I recall this little story about Charles Lindbergh when he flew across the Atlantic. An aide rushed to the President's office and shared the news with the President saying, "Charles Lindbergh has flown across the Atlantic single-handedly." The President said "That is nothing special. Tell him to try flying with a committee!" Of course I am not suggesting that we all sing solos. It is always easier to sing solos. It always stands out better if we sing solos. But there is no harmony in a solo. Let us try to sing a duet, or even better, let us all contribute to the choir of God.

When the Lord sent out His disciples He commanded them to be wise as serpents and harmless as doves. If I look back on some of our own approaches to China, if I study some of the approaches of some other organizations towards reaching China for Christ, I must honestly and shamefully say, we have been as dumb as doves and as harmful as serpents. We know literature can create either a good impact or a bad impact. We know literature can create either a good image or a bad image. Let us be sure that the Christian literature supplied to our brothers and sisters, to those that we love, inside China, is at least as good in content, in quality, in printing as those they see every day in China. Christ deserves the best. And the suffering Church inside China deserves the best.

China today is the most print-conscious nation on earth. The printed page, for them, is one of the most accepted means of communication. Far, far more of the available resources of the Christian community worldwide need to be pooled together, need to be worked together, need to be made available together to meet this gigantic challenge. I firmly believe that literature can no longer be treated as a mere tool of evangelization. I rest in the declaration of the Lord Jesus Christ Himself concerning one condition for his second coming, "And the Gospel must first be published among all nations."

Chapter 8

Radio

By Rev. Kenneth Lo

Broadcasting is the most popular medium in China right now. We have to use this medium to present a Christian message to the multitudes of people inside China. China is increasing its production in radios, not only in quantity but in quality, too. In fact, one of our staff last month just picked up a Communist-made radio in one of the Chinese department stores in Hongkong. It could receive the signal coming out from our new medium wave station DWRS and it came out quite well. Chinese high school students in China are taught sometimes in one special lesson to make radios themselves. One of our staff who came from China, and who has served more than two years with us, made a wonderful contribution to our studio. He himself made a very good short-wave studio. Another staff member gave up a very well paid job to join us as a full-time scriptwriter. He has travelled in more than 15 provinces in China, and gave us a very good report of the reception there.

Most Chinese, I feel, are very happy with overseas programs, even though they are illegal. Many people in China try very hard to tune into overseas programs partly as a change from incessant propaganda. Yet we need more than this knowledge as broadcasters. We have to believe in Christian broadcasting, and to talk about strategy in Christian broadcasting we have to talk about faith. What is our faith? Is it liberal theology? Is it the theology that believes Chairman Mao is the savior of China and that the quotations of Chairman Mao are the Bible for the Chinese? Such a faith thinks that China, at this time, needs no salvation, since they already have it. No one denies the material achievements, the improvements in the livelihood among the Chinese people. But the Chinese still need salvation. They still need a Savior. No matter whether Chinese are inside or outside China they are all sinners. So the radio message for China from us should be the Gospel and not just mere entertainment, or something that can be picked up from Radio Peking. I speak for FEBC, but we are no monopoly and all of us in the field of China broadcasts need total mobilization of all possible efforts to bring the message more effectively to the Chinese.

China needs more radio broadcasting, and more Bibles. If we don't cooperate, the radio ministry will be too expensive for us alone. For instance, in Hongkong, FEBC has just one program studio. In order to operate this studio we must have at least US$10,000 a month. But we have to pay power bills for our four different stations too. I have some figures from my brother, Fred Magbanua. He told me that the power bill for the Manila shortwave station and the DWRS medium wave station alone will cost US$21,000 per month. Now this is too much for FEBC, too much for the little group of churches and Christians that are supporting FEBC. We need co-operation in this gigantic ministry. In fact I am longing for some kind of co-operation among missions. FEBC is right now beaming the Gospel message daily to the Mainland from four different stations. Two of these are shortwave and the other two are medium wave. These four stations are located in three different countries. But may I remind you that when we think of the radio message to China, we should not think only in terms of shortwave. FEBC is now covering the whole land of China with medium wave, with its Korean station broadcasting to the north of China and the DWRS station in the Philippines broadcasting to the south.

Other organizations are also very energetic. TEAM has a very good radio station in Korea, but sad to say, we have heard that they are probably going to cease operation in the near future. There is RVOG, a radio station in Africa, and they have done a very good job, but owing to technical problems they have suspended their broadcasting ministry recently. I hope they can resume this ministry soon and join us later because they are right in the heart of the continent and we can co-operate well. Trans World Radio, TWR, is starting a new station on American soil. This will be helpful to us, too. There is co-operation among stations, among missions. In the Hongkong studio we are producing programs for nine sponsors and these nine sponsors are supporting us to produce 14 different programs. The Bible Society is asking us to produce in both Mandarin and Cantonese. The Overseas Missionary Fellowship, formerly known as the China Inland Mission, really has a heart for China and it is supporting a very good program called, "Golden Age." The Norwegian Lutheran Mission is very helpful. It not only supports our program, but also gives a very well-trained man on loan to us as our Program Director. The broadcasting ministry, I must tell you, will be more important in the future. It is important now. Even though China will be even more and more open in the future, and even though we may have thousands of Christians going in to preach the Gospel, still we need the radio. China's 900 million are too many for personal evangelism alone. We do not want to put all our eggs in the same basket. The situation in S.E. Asia has been changing very rapidly, and we must sit down and think so that China will not be deprived of the Gospel message by radio at any time in the future. I have mentioned many missions, many societies involved in the broadcasting work. I have not mentioned any single indigenous Chinese organization that is actively involved in radio programs. Should we do something about this? Should the Chinese churches and Chinese Christians make this more their own ministry?

We need also to cooperate in the production of programs. If we cooperate we can come up with more and better programs. We must realize that FEBC or any other station broadcasting to China competes with Radio Peking, with VOA, with BBC and even with Radio Hongkong. Some popular music from Hongkong is very attractive to the Chinese in Canton. How about the music from FEBC? We need better quality programs. Hence we need more qualified, trained staff. In fact, none of our full-time program staff in Hongkong has adequate professional training in the area of radio communications. We look forward to having seminary graduates from overseas who have the heart to reach the China Mainland come back to Hong Kong to help us with our programming. If they don't have training in radio, it is not a great problem. We can send them to another school to receive such training. Then they can come back and help us to make our programs more effective. We look forward to having more production centers, too.

We definitely need more active involvement from the Chinese churches. I praise the Lord for the wonderful involvement from many of our Western friends. But the Chinese churches are not involved enough. They are not active enough. For example, the Hong Kong studio is not yet self-supporting. Where are the Chinese churches and where are the Chinese Christians? It would be sad if the Communists said that a missionary-related organization was still subsidized by foreign funds. We need more involvement from gifted Chinese youth. We need script writers who can come up with meaningful scripts. We need announcers who can come up with standard Mandarin. I can speak Mandarin, but you may feel it is horrible, and I could never make a Mandarin program myself. We need standard Mandarin, but it is not easy to get it. It is not easy to get it from Mainland China because those refugees coming out from China are usually not Christians. It is not easy to get standard Mandarin from Taiwan. Mandarin speakers there are supposed to be under military training and the country won't let them go easily. We need more Mandarin-speaking announcers. If any Chinese now is preparing for a life work in China evangelism, I urge you, please consider this radio ministry. We can come up with some seminary courses that will make you the man or woman we need.

I became a Christian 14 years ago and then a year later I was called by God into the full-time ministry. After I finished my seminary education and also college education, my church called me back to be their pastor. Well that's fine, I know their needs, so I went back. But I told them very clearly that my call is not to be a pastor to look after the people in the church. It is good job, it is important, I love the church, but I do not believe that this is my job. I have had a certain feeling in my heart that God was calling me to preach to the Chinese people. I told the church board very frankly, and they did not argue with me. Last year I came full-time with FEBC. My church at that time had not got an ordained pastor, but they understood very clearly and could not argue with me because in the church I had been preaching very clearly again and again concerning reaching out to China, sending out the Gospel to them through the radio or any other possible means. What they have done is to try to retain as much of my time as possible. But they released me. You see, everybody can be involved. Everybody can do something for China. Everybody can pray for China.

Finally, let me just recount to you a little incident. Recently, a Christian woman left Hong Kong to visit China. She visited Canton and Shanghai to pay a special visit to her relatives. Before she left, she especially asked her pastor to pray very hard for her because she was trying to do some evangelistic work among her relatives. She reported to us that people were listening to FEBC radio in Canton and in Shanghai. But there was one incident that is quite significant. When she was in Shanghai, she was walking with her relatives to a government office. She knew perfectly well that her relative was not a Christian. Yet her relative told her, "We have been tuning in to overseas radio and we are very happy with FEBC broadcasting. Would you like to come tonight to our room so that we can listen to the radio together?" Well, of course, this woman went and six or seven of them stayed together. They had to close the room and listen carefully and concentrate as much as possible in order to tune to FEBC. But they listened regularly. Isn't this something? This Christian woman spoke to them more clearly about the message and asked them to make a decision. And so these people came to the Lord through a combination of personal evangelism and radio broadcasting. One thing is very significant. We have been producing Shanghainese programs for just 15 minutes a day, and have been thinking that this won't be effective. But these people in Shanghai, told the woman, "We love our dialect." So, they waited very late at night to tune to these 15 minutes of Shanghainese. They loved their mother tongue. This Christian woman went back to Hong Kong and especially requested her pastor to contact our office to enable her to come to give her testimony to us. She told us, "I understand that it is difficult for you people to be in this ministry. You need faith. You are practising through the microphone. You are speaking to a vacuum before your eyes. You don't know the response. So, I have just come to tell you that people are listening to the radio. Don't be discouraged. Don't give up and go on." Prayer is essential. Intercessors are absolutely necessary to bring the people inside China to Jesus Christ. This made me wonder whether FEBC would be wise to cease producing programs in the Chinese dialects.

Can I suggest something. I recently came across literature appealing for intercession for the Chinese and for the evangelization of China. The slogan was, "Let us have the tenth for the quarter." That means, all Christians are requested to put aside the tenth of every month. The tenth of every month, to the Chinese, means something else too. This ten symbolizes the cross, and will remind us how Jesus was crucified and laid down His body for all men. So, this slogan requests us to put aside specially the tenth of every month for the quarter of the world's population. This is good, isn't it? Have you started praying for China? But then, if we pray just one day in a month for the Chinese, it is insufficient. Why not pray more?

Chapter 9

Research Information Training

By Dr. Theodore Marr

Many of you are asking, "How can we share information about China?" I wonder what motivates you, or what prompts you to ask such a question? If you ask this purely from a practical point of view I must say that I believe no lasting good will come from attempts to share together what we know. There is only one basis for co-operation and that is the spiritual basis. Without a spiritual foundation I personally do not believe we can co-operate at all. I would like to turn to Philippians two, verses one to eleven. Everytime we read this passage in church or talk about it I am almost certain that we apply it only to individuals. We talk about being "likeminded" and having "the same love" between ourselves and our friends, between ourselves and the deacons, between ourselves and another man or woman in the church. Yet I entreat you today to look at this passage, not from the personal aspect, which we evangelicals have tended solely to look at, but from a group ethical point of view. Our problem is, we have forgotten the relationship between groups. I believe God is speaking to us in this conference, not only on an individual basis, but on a group basis.

Paul begins this passage by saying there are four pre-requisites before you can unite and co-operate. These four pre-requisites are, first, are you willing to cheer one another in Christ? Has any organization here cheered another organization in Christ recently? Have we cheered another one because a radio is hard to get, or because Bibles are hard to take into China? I wonder if we have done that. We must be concerned about other ministries at the same time as our own. Do we know what other people are doing in the China ministry? Second, you must be willing to love. Without the love of Christ there is no co-operation. How can we co-operate without that kind of foundation? We must build our foundation on the love of Jesus Christ. Third, we must witness through fellowship and communication. We see these pre-requisites clearly stated in the first verse of Philippians, chapter two. What is to communicate and to fellowship? It is to get to know each other. Yet we have groups that won't talk to each other. We have heads of organizations who refuse to communicate with each other. How can we talk about "Love China" unless we begin here, today, with this spiritual foundation? Fourth, willingness to express affection and sympathy. That is something about which you have to take a positive attitude, to take the initiative. It is·not that you wait around and sit around afraid to hurt somebody. With sympathy you go to another organization and say "How can we help you?" "What are your financial needs?" "Even though we also have needs, can we help you?" This is the spirit. These are the pre-requisites before we can co-operate.

Paul then goes on to say "complete my joy by having the same mind, the same love, the same accord." "The same mind," if you put it in another way is having the same ideology. We must begin with a foundation of theory, in this case, the same understanding of what preaching the Gospel really is, of how it is done. No wonder Communism has conquered so much of this world, because Communists have the same mind, the same ideology. Do we have it? Or are we so spread in our denominationalism, in our "isms," our doctrines, that there is no "same mind" at all? Where can we have co-operation? Second, "having the same love." What kind of love is it? Philippians goes on to say "the love of humility," the imitation of Christ's humility. That humility is the ultimate humility. From the highest position in the universe to the lowest position in mankind — to die on the cross. Can we be humble enough to say "My organization is no good. Yours is better?" If we have that kind of humility we begin to co-operate.

Finally there is having "one accord." That means unified action. Doing your own thing may be alright, except that what you do affects what others do also. What you do may close doors, instead of open them. Doing your own thing is not Christian. Having unified action is Christian. For all these points, Paul gives us many concrete suggestions. "Do nothing from selfishness or deceit, in humility count others better than yourselves." This does not just apply to individuals. We should count other organizations as better than our own. We have heard many reports here. None has said, "We are doing this job, but the other group is doing it better." How can we begin to talk about co-operation when we do not even have this spiritual foundation?

The problem of co-operation in the area on which I shall speak is research and information. We all know controlling information is controlling power. Whether you like it or not, that is the case. Therefore we hide information, because we want to have power, because we are more interested in our own interests. Co-operation begins with love, the same mind and the same action. Can we begin to look to the interests of others? Have this mind among yourselves, which you have in Christ Jesus. If we claim on the one hand that we have this mind in

Christ Jesus, but on the other hand we have not this mind among ourselves, we are liars. Christ emptied himself, taking the form of a servant. That is a very lowly form indeed. Our only way to share information effectively, to integrate it, interpret it, is to have unity in Christ with humility and to limit our purposes to enlarging the Kingdom of God.

Information today is not a simple thing. We are talking about information concerning China. I can assure you that there are few pieces of information that are passed on here today which you could not have picked up last week. All the information is there. Almost nothing is new. It's just that you did not know about it. What we as Christians concerned with China need is a good information storage recovering and retrieval system. And that takes some considerable skill. In the U.S. after the Sputnik went into orbit the Americans were a little worried that they would not get to the moon first. They pushed hard and they got there first. Intriguingly, one of the things that was pushed through Congress to win that race was the Ericson System. This was an enormous computer operation which integrated information from hundreds and hundreds of magazines and journals into one retrieval center. On a considerably smaller scale, that's what we Christians need: a computer information retrieval system that renders obsolescent our antiquated card systems. It blows your mind? Well, as a communications specialist let me suggest that within five years there will be home computer terminals on the market. To paraphrase — with apologies — Martin Luther: "Why should the devil have all the best technology?"

We must do research. There is no way that we can get out of that, because of the complexity of the situation in Mainland China. Without research a missionary can come to a new country thinking that he can evangelize it, love it, because he thinks in the same way he did wherever he was before. It's foolish, isn't it? Years ago through missionary training that man or woman had to learn customs and habits of his own country. Even if the language is the same, however, that hardly guarantees communication, I have trouble communicating. I remember on the first day when the Hong Kong delegates came in, they spoke Hong Kong English and the Filipinos spoke Filipino English. Even the names never got straight. We must understand the national concepts, national culture, and this is not easy by remote control. There is no way that anyone of us can get into China and learn about it from within. If we are going to train so many people and demand that one of the most important criteria of training is to visit China first and learn the language and learn the customs, we might as well forget about training. That kind of training just isn't possible. We must understand the reality of the situation and work within it.

There are many levels of co-operation and co-ordination. First of all we can begin by information exchange. But again I caution you, until you have that spiritual basis it is not even possible to exchange one piece of information. We can never even begin. Second, we can share projects. What projects? Well, cultural and social projects, to begin with. We have heard much discussion here of linguistic differences, language, meaning, cognitive differences between Chinese and Chinese, not to mention Chinese and foreigners. I am Chinese, but that does not lend me automatic access to the social and cultural actuality of the People's Republic. I believe there are tremendous cultural barriers to overcome. Language structure, for example. If any of you older Chinese read the *People's Daily* you know that it is awful going. Why, you can't even get through the first sentence! What about the social structure, the societal tension? In every society there is tension. Granted the family unit still remains in China, but does that family unit, in its present existence, fight for some sort of loyalty within itself along with loyalty to the commune, to the unit? What is that loyalty? I believe it is extremely important for us to understand that, if we are to meet with human emotion and human need, we must deal with China and the Chinese at that level. These are just two projects we can try out, and there are hundreds of others. We can work on these projects together.

Another instance of co-operation. Information is getting bigger. There is now a worldwide problem of information pollution. The biggest problem in academic circles today is, how do you know what is a good piece of information? What is a reliable piece of information? Much information is seen from our own preconceived attitudes and perspectives. Each one of us has that kind of weakness. How do we get over that? How do we assess accurate facts about China? We must share in information assessment because no Christian organization by itself can cope with the amount of work needed.

We must also share in training. My heart just pours out when a brother from Thailand and a sister from Tanzania talk about how they work. I wish that we could gather this experience together and pool this experience, so that they, through their experiences, could train us. How can we, through our own limited resource of experience, think that we can train everybody? We do not have the humility of Christ. Furthermore, in training there are so many levels. It takes people who can understand the whole economic and social system to interpret personal experience, and find out why that experience works for one individual, but may not work for another individual. Training comes at the cognitive, the effective, the experiential level, and you can name them all. We must get at this and work at it. We ought to share, we ought to publish our training schedules, so that we could attend each others.

Lastly, we should have long-term development plans. Long-term! Have you thought about what is going to happen in 10 years? You think about tomorrow, maybe. Or in 20 years? We should think about the kind of things we want to do in the China field in 10 years, then we can be prepared now. Long-term projects are extremely difficult to devise and work out. It takes a lot of co-operation. To build up a good information system takes at least five years. You will not be able to really use it until five years from now. Yet if there is a lack of co-operative spirit, without the same mind and the same accord, how can we talk about five years? In five years we might still be fighting each other. Why should I give you information? I am tempted to ask always. You may store it in your department, in your organization, and I may never be able to get that information back. How much better, right now, to pool our resources, to co-operate in research, in training, in information exchange! The co-operation can without question take place because we are free to co-operate. But there is one thing which must come first: the spiritual foundation Paul tells us about in the second chapter of Philippians.

Chapter 10

Love China Vision

By Rev. David Adeney

I think it is true to say that there are three different views of China. We find three different types of reports coming out of China concerning the Church. We sometimes read in the paper of those who go to China and they see the Church is closed and they say, "Christianity is finished." They see the church buildings with the cross taken away and being used for secular purposes. The cross, indeed, is no longer on the church buildings. It is upon the lives of individual Christians. We cannot blame non-Christians who come to the conclusion that there is no sign of Christianity. Sometimes, even Christians who go become almost depressed. I was talking to one man who had been travelling in China with a team of doctors. He saw the tremendous sense of independence. And his impression was, here are people who have accomplished so much and they no longer need God. I'm reminded of this slogan that we had when we were living under the Communists, "Don't worship heaven, don't worship earth, only worship the efforts of the people." You know that there is a tremendous emphasis upon the efforts of the people and this Christian friend of mine said, "I'm beginning to become depressed." Then, in a wonderful way, there was a dramatic theater show on the last day which ended with a very bright light shining, and everybody going down on their knees. Then, somebody brought on stage a portrait of chairman Mao Tse-tung. My friend suddenly saw that still, the great need in China is for someone who will meet the spiritual hunger of the hearts of men and women.

There is another report coming from China. There are those who feel that the important thing in China is not the number of Christians. A friend of mine met someone coming out of Shanghai and asked, "What about the Church in Shanghai?" And to his dismay, the answer was, "I'm not interested in the numbers of Christians or in Christians meeting together for fellowship. I'm only impressed in the tremendous changes taking place in China." For some, salvation has come to mean deliverance from oppression, from injustice and inequality. As for the revolution in China, it is regarded as salvation in history. People with this outlook see the great progress made in material wealth. They feel God's presence is not to be seen in little groups of Christians worshipping together, but rather, in the great structural changes in society. Christianity to them is the application of the Christian ethic, not necessarily under the name of Christ. One young Catholic visitor said, "It is clear that the China which broke the hearts of the missionaries has accepted the Spirit of Christ from another source, namely Marxism. If the Chinese have, indeed, created a society with more faith, more hope, and more love than the Christian West, then they deserve not only attention but allegiance." Then, he added: "We must follow where the Spirit blows." And Professor Joseph Needham, who is sometimes described as a Christian and a Marxist said, "I think China is the only Christian country in the world today, in spite of its absolute rejection of all religion. It is," he said, "where Christ is to be found, where the good are and where good things are done." That means appreciating what is happening in China today. I felt deeply disturbed when I read such statements. I know good writers are concerned about social issues in China. Certainly, we must appreciate all that has been done to alleviate suffering. But it is a terrible tragedy when people have no concept of what God purposes to do through His Church, when they lose sight of God's great purpose in the Lord Jesus Christ, when they fail to see that there is no salvation apart from our Lord Jesus.

The third view is represented at this conference. We recognize that God permitted the revolution to take place and is able to work even through the actions of men who do not know Him. We know that in the history of the people of God, there have been many times when those who have not believed in God have been used as instruments to fulfill God's purposes. And sometimes they have been used to bring judgement upon those who have practised injustice and oppression. But at the same time, we affirm our conviction that God's great purpose for His Church has not changed. In spite of all the failures of the past, God has called out for Himself amongst the millions of China a people whom He has redeemed and through whom He has revealed His love and His full salvation. And God has entrusted to those who may be despised, maybe few in number, the Gospel of His Son. There are those in China today who believe that every knee must bow, and every tongue confess that Jesus Christ is Lord to the Glory of God.

Now, as we think of the future, we first of all must understand the nature of the Church in China today. Then, we must see the lessons that it is teaching us. And then, we must seek to understand the action that God would have us to take. First of all, look at the Church in China. It is a Church that has been purified by suffering. Most of the outward trappings of the institutional Church have been taken away. We often think of the Church in terms of our

Sunday services, of the buildings that we use, and the various institutions of the Church. That has disappeared in China. And the Church is unknown. To join the Church is not easy. It was in Shanghai, recently, that someone was asking about becoming a Christian. And the first thing that was said to him was, "If you want to become a Christian, you must be ready to suffer." It's quite clear that people do not join the Church for ulterior motives. There is, therefore, a reality in the life of the Church. You do not find, as we are used to saying, "Those with a name but no reality."

The faith of those who join the Church in China today is constantly being tested. They face the loneliness and indoctrination courses. Some of them have spent years in prison or labor camps. I recently talked to a mother, whose daughter has just been recently released after 15 years in prison. And that mother said to me, "My daughter is just as keen a Christian today as that day, when as a student, she was arrested and put into prison." A young Christian who had been in a commune all her life described to me something of the loneliness, and yet of the wonder, the comfort of God's Word. She was loaned a copy of the Scriptures for one month. One day, she was reading that Scripture and the person who had given her the Bible suddenly came in when she was reading it. He was seriously alarmed. He said, "You were reading it openly. Is there no danger that it might be lost." She said, "No. I'm not afraid. My neighbors know I'm a Christian and they respect me." Think of the joy of reading a Bible. You can only have it for such a short time, then, it must be passed on. In that Church in China today, there are those who in a very real way are experiencing the comfort of the Holy Spirit. The Holy Spirit is teaching them through the Word of God. The Holy Spirit is miraculously making His presence and power felt in their lives.

We have heard of some of the sad experiences in the early days in Communist China when Christians denounced Christians. But thank God there are those today who know that they can trust their fellow believers. They do not belong to a privileged class. They show their love, the reality of their Christian life, through their love to others and the quality of their life. One of the members of this conference sometime ago told me of an experience of a Christian in a hotel. In that hotel in South China, he noticed that there was a lady who was cleaning the floor. There was such a look of love and graciousness on the face of that person. And he waited until there was an opportunity to speak to her alone. He said, "Are you a Christian?" And her reply was, "Yes. I cannot say much but I seek, through the life I'm living, to reveal the Lord Jesus."

Now, what is the message that God is giving

us through His Church? I think we must realize that there are important lessons coming from China which must be received by the Church throughout the whole world. Our vision for the future must include the influence of the Church in China upon the Church in other countries. It's tragic if we fail to learn the lessons that God is teaching through the experience in China. Christians in Vietnam, in Laos, in Cambodia are going through trials similar to those which their brethren have passed through in China. Even in Africa. I just received a letter from Ethiopia. And someone who had been reading my book about the student witness under Communism said, "Our students are going through the same kind of indoctrination courses. We desperately need help and advice how they can continue their witness." I was quite surprised to receive a letter from Portugal. And it said, "We have already translated your book." And they sent me copies later on. Students need to know how to face up to these things.

The message of the Christians in China should come to the whole world. Surely, it must be part of the work in this conference to overcome the indifference and the lethargy which prevents the Church throughout the world from hearing the call from their Christian brethren in China. There are important lessons coming from those 25 years of the experience of Christians in China. I think, first of all, that we are reminded

again of the sovereignty of God. And we can
trust the loving power and concern of our God
for His own people whatever the trials may be.
Revolution may close the door to foreign
missionaries. But as we have heard, the door is
not closed in China. Today, I believe that it's
going to be mainly through the Chinese that the
Gospel is coming to China. The Lord may enable
some from other countries to enter China in
different ways for a quiet witness in their
various professions, but, the main witness is
going to be through our Chinese brothers and
sisters. That doesn't mean that others do not
have a responsibility, as we shall see. Another
thing I believe we are learning from China is the
example of faithfulness in the midst of persecution. I have been so stirred by hearing of some,
who in the midst of great troubles, have
remained true to their Lord. I remember hearing
of one man who had the opportunity of coming
out of the labor camps where he was, but he
would not in any sense compromise his faith.
And his sister told me of the tremendous joy,
when in a way that I cannot explain, that man
who has been without a Bible for years, was
given a Bible. But when we listen to faithfulness
in the midst of suffering, are we not often ourselves rebuked for our inconsistency? I sometimes think to myself, "I can pray that Chinese,
my Chinese brethren, may stand true and not
deny our Lord whatever the cause," and yet, I

may be unwilling to make the smallest sacrifice. I heard someone say a tragic remark. He said, "Christianity will not do for Asia. It's not sufficiently sacrificial." I'm reminded again of the words of a man so well known in Chinese literature, Hu Shih. As he met a group of nominal Christians he said to them, "If I believed one-tenth of what you say you believe, I would be ten times more enthusiastic." We see people giving everything for the sake of the Gospel. And we are content to live an easy life.

The need today is not necessarily for great crowds of people. The Church, the value of the Church and the strength of the Church, is not judged by the numbers who come to the Sunday morning service. It depends on the spiritual quality. We find that in Communism, there's tremendous emphasis upon the trained cadre. Is it not true that unless a Church has got a band of people utterly dedicated, knowing the power of God in their lives, that Church will not really stand and glorify God? Our vision for the future must, therefore, be the training of dedicated disciples. We need to see laymen being trained. We need to see in every Church that there are elders, there are those who are learning the Word of God and becoming men and women with power in their lives, who are storing God's Word in their hearts and are seeking to understand the application of God's Word to the society in which they are living. The Church in China is robbed of its outward leaders, robbed of a regular clergy, yet is becoming truly a Kingdom of Priests, meeting in homes and experiencing the reality and the fellowship of the Son of God. Then, I believe, we must train people not only that they may become strong in the Scriptures and in the knowledge of God's power in their lives, but also, that they understand what's happening in the world. I sometimes feel that we are often very superficial. We don't really get down to study. We don't really have the answer when we meet people who speak out the glory of a materialistic or of an atheistic philosophy of life. When I was in China, I remember looking out in the morning and seeing all those groups of students studying. I believe, in China today, that everybody is supposed to have ten hours of political study a week. The students have far more than that. That is political study.

I've said again that we must learn that the Church must not be dependent upon one man. A church that is largely dependent upon the pastor and confined to a building center program is very vulnerable. And that's why I believe that in every church there should be the developing of small groups and the starting of other smaller churches, so that anytime the large meetings cannot be held, there will be these little groups continuing to witness. In a university, just recently, all large meetings were banned. This was in Malaysia. And there have been times when very large Christian fellowships could not have any of their regular activities and had to find out what it means to continue witnessing one by one in little groups. That may happen in other places.

There is one other thing that I believe we must learn. The Christians in China have given us an example of being integrated into society. They know what it is to have to apply what they believe to the problems of the society in which they live. I believe that very, very often the Christians are living apart from the problems of society. There are large sections of the population that we are not reaching. One of the leaders in Singapore said to me recently, "The Christians in Singapore — almost all come from 30% of the population. We find Christians enjoying relatively high standards of living. They give little thought to the gaps between the have's and the have-not's. Imprisoned in a kind of middle class mentality, they're making very little impact upon the thousands and thousands in the factories." I think sometimes we are put to shame by the emphasis in China of "Serve the people." I think that if a church neglects that part of the Gospel which emphasizes "preaching the Good News to the poor, releasing the captives, the recovering of sight to the blind and liberty for those who are oppressed" we may find ourselves totally unprepared to live in a Communist society. This is not to say that social service prepares the Church to live under Communism. The Church ministers to the poor and needy, not in order to prepare for a possible revolution, but to fulfill the command given by the Lord Jesus. For no amount of social service will ever make the Church acceptable to Communism. But if we are not understanding of the needs of multitudes on earth around us, whom we are not touching with the Gospel, then we are failing. I asked a young Christian dentist one day, "Why don't you go and set up a clinic in one of those very poor areas, where there are high rise apartments." And he said to me, "My colleagues will say I'll be an absolute fool to do that." And yet, brothers and sisters, unless we are going to see doctors and dentists and engineers and teachers and other professional people going out to a place where the need is greatest and are not seeking for their own good, surely, we're not worthy of the Gospel of Jesus Christ. We had one doctor at our discipleship training center. Before he came to us and when he graduated from the university, instead of going into a good position, he went out into one of the islands where there were no facilities at all and where the people had no medical service. And there, he set up a clinic to witness for Jesus Christ. So often, we wait for the government to scatter us. I have often said that in one country that there is a great blessing, the government insists that all the young teachers be sent out to rural areas and in that way, year after year, you get young teachers who are Christians bringing new life to the rural districts.

Finally, we must ask, "What is it that God would have us to do?" First of all, if I summarize again, I believe that the barrier of ignorance and indifference to what is happening in China must be broken down. I found it desperately sad when many, many churches and Chinese churches actually know very little at all of what's happening in China and have very little concern. It's impossible to keep alive prayer interest and concern without constant reminders and some information. We can only have fellowship with the Church in China if this ministry of intercession is maintained. I suggest that somehow the prayer letters that are coming out must be far more widely circulated. So often, we just have different little organizations sending out a few prayer letters whereas some of these materials should be shared and sent out as widely as possible. Secondly, I believe that we must thank God for all our Chinese brothers and sisters who are able to go into China. We should encourage them. And surely, there must be preparation. There must be the understanding of the ideology. There must be seminars and workshops. There must be the ability to identify the people with the people with whom they will live. We must realize that it's going to be very difficult in a sense, going from an urban situation and the high standards of living that we have in so many of our cities and then learning to adjust in the society of China today. There must indeed be an understanding of the desires and of the longings of the people in China. And for this reason, I believe that we must see much more research done. Surely, there's a need for Chinese evangelical scholars who will continue to study both the Scriptures and the current patterns of thought in China today. We have heard about the radio work. But we must also make every effort to make contact with those who come from China. I know a Chinese Christian doctor who made contact with doctors coming from China. A student Christian fellowship in one university is making contact with students who come from China. They are very fine people and these people are needing Christian friends. A Christian lecturer in another university has been put in charge of a group of students who come from China to study. Someone in this conference spoke to me of the fact that in some newspapers, jobs are being offered for people in China, teaching English and so on. And if there's an opportunity to go into China, why shouldn't Christians go in and take this opportunity? It was right during the Cultural Revolution that l said goodbye on the railway station in Kowloon to a Canadian scientist who had been invited by the Chinese government to visit China. He didn't have an easy time. He took his whole family in and there was one day when a banquet was arranged for him. And his friend, the leading scientist of the town, who had been showing him around was the one who had to speak at the banquet. My scientist friend said he had wonderful friendship with this man. But in that public banquet, this man had to make a very political speech, attacking the imperialist powers of the west, especially America. At the end of his speech, my friend stood up and he said, "I'm a scientist. I don't understand a great deal about politics." Then he said, "There's only one thing I want to say to you. I came to China with my family. I have one desire and that is, we as a family might show the love of Jesus Christ." It wasn't very much. But the one who made the speech came to him afterwards when they were alone. He said, "I want you to know I understand what you are saying." There are opportunities.

Chapter 11

Prayer and Action

By Rev. Rey Frame

What action should we take in response to all that we have seen and heard? I would suggest that one action that all of us can take is to begin praying. Prayer is an action that is very much needed. In James 5:16, the second statement in that verse, we read, "The effectual fervent prayer of a righteous man availeth much." Without prayer, truly no Christian missionary will be constrained by the love of Christ to run the risk of missionary work in China today. And without the right kind of prayer the man-made restrictions now inhibiting free evangelistic activity within the borders of China will not be removed and may actually become even more severely restricted. What then is the right kind of prayer? I submit that the right kind of prayer, if we really decide that Mainland China should be evangelized and evangelized soon, is the kind of prayer that the prophet Daniel prayed shortly before God inspired King

Cyrus to issue his famous decree that the Jewish captives in Babylon and elsewhere should at last be set free to return to their homeland, to rebuild the temple, so that the lamp of God that had been extinguished in the land of Israel for 70 years should once more be lighted in Jerusalem. Now what caused King Cyrus to do such a wonderful and totally unusual thing? It was because of an old man, probably in his 80's, Daniel. Daniel prayed the right kind of prayer at exactly the right time in world history. And God one hundred percent approved of that prayer and therefore God exercised His sovereign authority over the nation and brought about the result that Daniel had longed to see. In a short time, Daniel's people were set free to do what God wanted them to do.

Now, if we today can learn to pray the right kind of prayer, is there any reason why God should not, once more, set us free to do what our hearts already urge us to do for China? Let us now look briefly at the prophet Daniel's prayer life so that we can capture its significance clearly enough to give much thought to it later on. We learn here in a brief examination of Daniel's prayer life, how a righteous man or woman can actually move God to action by prayer alone. Chapters 9 and 10, in the prophecy of Daniel, describe one of the climaxes of Daniel's long prayer life. We see here how Daniel was able to move God, to move King

Cyrus and to do so by prayer alone. Time will not allow us this morning to read those two rather long chapters, chapters 9 and 10 of Daniel but we should read them privately when we have time.

In verse two of Chapter 9 of the book of Daniel, we notice that Daniel was driven to prayer on this occasion for his captive countrymen who were in Babylon together with him, and that this prayer was triggered by something Daniel had read in the Holy Scriptures. We read, "In the first year of his reign I Daniel understood by books (that is by reading some of the scrolls of Jeremiah's prophesies) the number of years, whereof the word of the Lord came unto Jeremiah the prophet, that God would accomplish 70 years in the desolations of Jerusalem." So those 70 years Daniel suddenly realized were just about complete. But were the Jews, living in Babylon, interested now in going back to the land of Israel to rebuild the temple and to establish the worship of Jehovah God in Israel and relight that lamp which had been extinguished for 70 years? The answer was that the people of Israel were not ready. They were not interested. They now loved things in Babylon. Few had any thoughts of returning to Israel. It was this sad fact that moved Daniel to begin fasting and praying for his cold and indifferent people. And he wept as he prayed and he kept on praying until an answer came from heaven.

But God's first answer, which we read about in chapter 9 of Daniel, was an answer that caused Daniel to feel more discouraged than ever. God gave Daniel the bad news that far from the Jews being now free to return to Israel and to set-up a· glorious kingdom like the kingdom that David and Solomon enjoyed and ruled over, far from that, they must still endure a total of 70 times 70 years of more trouble and more gentile oppression, 490 years of it all together before there was any hope. Well, that was bad news. Then, when we reach chapter 10, we see Daniel sometime later in a state of very deep depression. On this occasion, Daniel seemingly just waited for God. For 21 days he just waited for God but he did not say much. He groaned, he wept, but everytime God looked down, there was old Daniel still crying, still waiting for God, waiting for God's answer, waiting for God to overtake. Finally, after 21 days had expired, the Archangel, it probably was Gabriel, appeared to Daniel with God's answer, God's second answer. Gabriel explained why it was that there was a delay of 21 days before his prayer could be answered and Gabriel could arrive with God's answer. He said he had been held up by Satan's Prince of Persia who headed up the devil's invisible government behind the scenes exercising real control over the Kingdom of Persia which had just overthrown the Kingdom of Babylon a few years earlier. Now, as Daniel,

God's agent stayed down on earth, waited on God and wept for Israel and her liberation, as Daniel prayed, Gabriel and his forces were strengthened until Gabriel finally was able to route the forces of the Prince of Persia, that is, the Satanic Prince of Persia and was able to break through and bring the good news to Daniel and then go on to give God's message to some of the key leaders of the captured nation of Israel there in Babylon.

Now, what Gabriel said to Cyrus we don't know. But we can guess when we read King Cyrus' own report and I'll read that very briefly in Second Chronicles 36:22-23, "Now in the first year of Cyrus King of Persia, that the Word of the Lord spoken by the mouth of Jeremiah might be accomplished, the Lord stirred up the spirit of Cyrus King of Persia, that he made a proclamation throughout all his nation and put it into writing, saying, "Thus says Cyrus, King of Persia, All the Kingdoms of the earth hath the Lord God of Heaven given me; and He hath charged me to build Him a house in Jerusalem which is in Judah. Who is there among you of all his people? The Lord his God be with him and let him go up." Now notice this was in the first year of Cyrus; but Daniel got the second answer, that is, Gabriel came the second time in the third year of Cyrus. Now, why was Daniel so depressed and so discouraged three years after Cyrus had issued the edict that the people could return to Israel and rebuild the Temple? Cyrus seemed more concerned about building a Temple to God than the captives of Israel were concerned about that thing. So probably this second visit of Gabriel was a visit in which he spoke personally, dramatically to some of the great leaders, the priests and the political leaders of Israel. And when they had that personal visitation from Heaven, they woke up and they began to take action about returning to their homeland. That is why Daniel was depressed because his own people were not interested. Although the door was wide open, the king himself was standing behind them, willing to back them financially and every other way, and yet there was complete lethargy. That's what broke the old man's heart and he wept before God a further 21 days until God gave him a new message and things started to move.

Now, God has not changed. His promises have not weakened. So, if you and I know how to pray the right kind of prayer as Daniel did on that occasion, prayer that makes the principalities and powers of Satan helpless, as Daniel was down there praying, when those forces of the devil that were against Israel were bowed and Gabriel was able to come through, we shall prevail. Someone has said, "The world has yet to see what is accomplished by a saint upon his knees." As we are upon our knees, God will bind those forces that are behind the forces that are closing the doors to the Gospel today. That is the only way to open doors, for the Gospel to go forth, — binding the strong powers of darkness in the heavenly places that are controlling this earthly kingdom. As they are bound, the leaders of those kingdoms will be set free to do what God wants them to do. So, once again, the light of open teaching and open testimony to the Word of God may be lit in that great land of China as we pray.

Chapter 12

Intercession

By Rev. William Willis

I have been given the assignment of preaching to you on the subject of intercessory prayer. But I never preach without first asking God's blessing. If you will please bow your heads and close your eyes, just for a few moments, I will lead you in prayer.

"Oh God, our loving Heavenly Father, we, thy little children come to Thee. We will still learn of Thee. We desire to be better Christians. We want to know more about prayer. We want to pray more, so we ask Thee to speak to us through Thy Word. We thank Thee for the records of Holy men of God who knew how to pray and how to get answers from God. We, too, want to be able to pray and get answers from Thee. We live in a desperately, desperately wicked world, and Thy Church has a desperate need, too. A need for men and women who can really pray and call down answers from God, right out of the heart of God. So, bless us Lord, help me Lord, and glorify Thy great Name in our midst for Jesus sake and for Thy Glory and for Thy Glory alone. Amen."

Let us look together at the prophecy of Ezekiel, chapter 22, verse 30, "And I sought for a man among them that should make up the hedge and stand in the gap before me for the land, that I should not destroy it: but I found none." The statement made here does not necessarily mean that there were no praying people left in the whole of the world. In our Churches today, in our congregation, in this congregation, there are people who pray. In Ezekiel's day, we can assume that there were at least a small remnant of people who still believed in their God and made their prayers made known unto Him. But there was no one who cared enough, no one with a vision, no one who was alarmed, no one who cried aloud to God on behalf of the people. Could no one see the wickedness that was all about them? Priests and people, we are told, had forsaken God. Only a handful of people, it appears, still worshipped God, and still prayed to Him. No one, it seems, considered that the day of judgement must come. It might tarry, but it would come. And that day came. Not before God looked everywhere for a man who could intercede for the people. A man with vision, a man with a broken heart, a man who would at last lay down his own life that the people, the sinful people all around him, might once again turn to God.

Read the text again, verse 30 and verse 31. But first of all, let me point out that these two verses must never be separated. If you read verse 30, you must also read verse 31. We often hear verse 30 read. Many preachers quote it. But very rarely do we read or hear preachers quoting this 31st verse. Yet to overlook this verse is a great mistake. "And I sought for a man among them that should make up the hedge and stand in the gap before me for the land, that I should not destroy it: but I found none. Therefore — or because of this, on account of the fact that I could not find the man — therefore, have I poured out my indignation upon them; I have consumed them with the fire of my wrath: their own way have I recompensed upon their heads, saith the Lord God."

When God lights up these two verses that we have just read together, what effect do they have on you? I'll tell you what it does to me to read these two verses together. It humbles me deeply. Questions arise within me and they call for an answer. Am I a man of prayer? Do I care what becomes of sinners? Am I an intercessor? Have I a deep burning love in my soul for those who are lost and on their way to hell? Does it matter to me that so many are perishing? Do I in deed and in truth love China? Nine hundred million souls — in some books they would say more, in others less — and everyone of them has been bought with a price. Bought with a price. Not with silver or gold but with the precious blood of the Son of God, our Blessed Lord Jesus Christ. And everyone of them is precious in His Sight. Every Chinese, every Englishman, every American, every African, every person in every nation under the sun, is precious to the Lord Jesus Christ. You may not care what becomes of them, but He cares.

Dr. Joe Wert, one of England's great preachers half a century or so ago, used to tell this story. There was a young man in his congregation in whom he was very interested. He graduated from the university with the highest honor. He was a brilliant young man in many ways. His pastor and all his friends spoke of his wonderful future. And one day, he made an announcement that shocked everybody. He said he was going to Africa. God had called him. They pointed out that he was not too strong physically. They pointed out to him that with such a beginning, a wonderful future awaited him. In some walk of life he would make his mark and probably become famous. But he brushed them all aside and he went to Africa. A year later, he came home, broken in body. Dr. Joe Wert, his pastor, welcomed him gladly and planned for him a useful career in the church. The doctor was quite sure that he would soon settle down and forget all about Africa and its population. But it didn't happen that way. He was restless. He looked very troubled all the time. The doctor gave him duties to perform in the church and he performed them well. But it was quite evident to everybody that he was a very unhappy young man. One day, his pastor took him aside and asked him, "What's the matter? You're busy and yet you're uneasy all the time, you're unhappy. What's the matter with you?" And immediately, the tears began to run down his face and he answered. His answer was, "I can't sleep at night for thinking of them. I can't sleep at night for thinking of them." Could you say that? The millions of souls that are on the way to hell, walking along the broad road that leads to destruction. Do you care enough about them? Could you truthfully say, "I can't sleep at night for thinking of them." There is one thing of which all of us are very sure. God and His Son, our Blessed Lord Jesus Christ Himself, has been looking down upon us in this meeting. The Holy Spirit has been here working in our midst. He has been moving among us, touching this one and that one. And what has our response been? Have we been complacent or compassionate? Complacency is a deadly thing. Complacency is a grave mistake as seen in the life of any Christian. And yet it is so common. I go to a lot of churches. I preach to a lot of congregations. And the one thing I notice is, that so many of them are complacent, satisfied. They say they love Jesus, they say they're filled with the Holy Spirit, and they are always coming together in meetings. Meeting after meeting after meeting. They're so pleased with themselves. So complacent. It seems that, out there in the world, they never think of those who are lost without God and without hope in the world.

I want to share II Chronicles, chapter 7, verse 14 with you. "If my people, which are called by my name, shall humble themselves and pray, and seek my face, and turn from their wicked ways; then will I hear from heaven, and will forgive their sin, and will heal their land."

What God is really saying here is, if my people will, then I will. The onus is upon us. God is waiting for us. Listen for a moment to the prophet Jeremiah. He had vision and the burden that vision brings. But he knew what to do.

In Jeremiah 13, verse 17, we read, "My soul shall weep in secret places." And God saw him there. God saw every tear and heard every word. And one day God came to him and said to him, "Refrain thy voice from weeping and thine eyes from tears for thy work will be rewarded."

Do you ask me, "What is an intercessor?" An intercessor is a man who prays and weeps in the secret place of prayer until God stoops down and dries his tears. In Hebrews 5, verse 7 we read that, Jesus "in the days of His flesh, offered up prayers and supplications with strong crying

187

and tears." Let me ask you, when you prayed about Love China '75, did you pray with strong crying and tears? Have you recently read the story of that great man, Moses, the story that is told in Exodus, chapter 32? We all know the story, but let me refresh your memory. Moses had been up in the mount with God for 40 days and 40 nights. The people below, on the plain, got tired of waiting for him. They even spoke what they felt in their hearts. They said, "We don't know what's become of this man, Moses. He's been gone now for 40 days and 40 nights, and we don't know where he is." Then they said a terrible thing. "Let us make gods that are gold!" And all of us here know the story of the Golden Calf they made and bowed down to and worshipped. And when Moses came down from the mount with the two tablets of stone upon which God had written His Holy Law, and saw and heard for himself, those two tablets of stone fell from his hands and were broken. I don't know how Moses felt in that moment when he actually saw God's people dancing around a Golden Calf. But he went down into the plain and he dealt with them. He called out to them, "Who is on the Lord's side?" And there were some, there were some, who had not participated in that idol worship and still believed in God. And Moses said, "Consecrate yourselves afresh this day to the Lord." And then we read in verse 30, Exodus 32, "And it came to pass on the morrow that Moses said unto the people, ye have sinned a great sin: and now I will go up unto the Lord; peradventure I shall make an atonement for your sin." Let me read the next two verses, 31 and 32. And listen carefully, will you? "And Moses returned unto the Lord and said, 'Oh, this people have sinned a great sin and have made them gods of gold. Yet now, if thou wilt forgive their sin and,' " — and after that word sin, there's a dash. It signifies that Moses has broken down. His heart is breaking. He can't go on, he can't continue his prayer. And then when he could recover himself a bit, this is what he said, "And if not, blot me, I pray thee, out of thy book which thou has written." Well, you have just listened to the heart cry of an intercessor. And what he says reminds us that, if we would emulate him, there's a price to be paid. It costs to be an intercessor. You can pray and pray and pray and pray and it won't cost you anything. But if you intercede with God, it will cost you something. All intercessors have paid a great price.

In the New Testament, we read, in the Epistle to the Romans, in chapter 8, we read about this man rejoicing in the fact that nothing, nothing will ever separate him from "the love of God which is in Christ Jesus our Lord." And then, only two verses later, we find him saying, "I have great heaviness and continual sorrow in my heart. And he calls upon the Holy Ghost to witness that he is speaking the truth. "I have great heaviness and continual sorrow in my heart. For I could wish that I were accursed from Christ, for my brethren, my kinsmen according to the flesh." In one breath he says, nothing can separate him from the love of God which is in Christ Jesus. In the very next breath he says, there's one thing I could wish myself accursed from Christ for, if thereby, my brethren, my kinsmen might be saved.

I was saved during the great Welsh Revival of 1904 and 1905, the Great Revival of Wales. Wales is a part of the British Isles. It's west of England. In 1904 and 1905, Wales experienced a mighty revival in which tens of thousands of people were brought to Jesus. And I was one of them. I was one of them. It is almost impossible to describe the events that took place during that mighty revival. Strong men fell down in the streets crying to God for mercy. How did it begin? There was a young man called Evan Roberts. He was only a coal miner. He went to the coal pit everyday, like most of the young men of this time, to make a living. He was sitting, one morning, in the pulpit of a church for he was to preach that day. He was a lay preacher. His face was covered by his hands, but the tears were trickling through his fingers. Suddenly, without any warning, a young lady rose in the congregation and began to sing. And the mighty Spirit of God swept over that

church. A man sitting over there on the left
suddenly rose up, threw his arms above his head
and cried out, "God have mercy on me." And
that was characteristic of the revival. A deep
sense of sin, of a conviction of sin. But oh, what
a mighty revival that was. In the first six months
of that revival, 150,000 newly converted people
asked for permission to be members in one or
other of the participating churches. All classes
and conditions of people were converted. That
little church where it began was never closed,
day or night, for two years. And day and night
for two years, people were crowding into it and
finding salvation. I remember this one story
particularly, a man, miner, a coal miner, a
notoriously wicked man, whose mouth was
filled with cursing and blasphemy. Even some of
the other miners, before they were converted,
wouldn't work with him. One day this Godless
man, working down in the pit, suddenly, to
everybody's astonishment cried out, "God have
mercy on me," and he fell on his face. They
helped him up to the pit shaft, they put him in
the cage, took him to the surface, took him to
the nearest church, and there, he found Jesus
Christ as his personal savior. The most wicked
man in the whole of Wales.

All the bars were closed, the dance halls
were closed, the theaters were closed, the
gambling dens were closed, the houses of prosti-
tution were closed, all these places where men

had flocked before were closed. There were no customers. Instead of going to these places, they were flocking to the house of prayer.

And the hills and the valleys of Wales resounded, as they sang the praises of God. You know, the Welsh have always been proud of their singing. They are great singers. If you heard that chorus of men singing in Wales, it would make you tingle. There's nothing like it.

Before they were saved, before their revival, they would sing as they went to work and sing as they came home from work, but they were ribald sounds, songs of the world. But as they got converted in the revival, they began to sing the songs of Isaiah, "Guide me, Oh thou great Jehovah," and other wonderful, wonderful songs.

I've chosen my message because I feel the need for it. The need, not of men who can pray — there are a lot of men here who can pray, there are a lot of women here who can pray — but, I am wondering, I am wondering, is there an intercessor here? Is there a man like Evan Roberts here, the man God used to lead that great revival? I visited Wales some years after the revival. I was invited by the Rev. Sydney Evans, a young man who, during the revival, was the constant companion of Evan Roberts. Evan Roberts had departed from the scene. It seems that God raised him up to lead that great revival because after the revival, as it ebbed away, he disappeared.

But his friend, Sydney Evans, went on into the ministry. He was the pastor of a church in South Wales. He wrote to me one day and he asked me, would I go and conduct an evangelistic campaign in his church? So I went. And one day, we were sitting together in his study and it suddenly occurred to me, if there is any man living who can give me the secret of Evan Roberts, the secret of the Welsh Revival, this is the man.

So I turned to him and I said, "Sydney, what was the secret of Evan Roberts? What was the secret of the Welsh Revival?" He thought for a moment or two, then he said, "A number of us young men used to, after our day's work, go home and clean up and have a meal, and then we would go up on the mountainside, 15 or 16 of us, and we would pray. We were praying for revival. The churches were cold. No one was getting converted. And these young men longed for a revival. So night after night, night after night, they went up on the mountainside and prayed for a revival." My friend, Sydney Evans, said to me, "and Evans, you know, Evan Roberts, he would be with us, but he wouldn't stay, he would quietly steal away and go a little further up the mountain. And when our prayer meeting broke up, I used to go to find him. And I knew where to look and I would find him, laying on the ground, his face to the ground I would find him, with the tears running down his face. And I would hear him sobbing out, "Oh God, break me, break me, break me." God broke him. As I said before, there's a price to be paid.

That we desperately need a revival, everybody will agree I am sure. And nobody longs more than I do, to see the mighty Holy Spirit sweeping through meetings and sweeping men and women into the Kingdom. And I sometimes seem to hear God saying, "I sought for a man, but I found none." There is a price to be paid. But may I remind you of the words King David uttered 3,000 or more years ago. Do you know what he said? "Shall I offer unto the Lord that which hath cost me nothing?"

What does your praying cost you? I am here tonight as God's ambassador. I am here tonight to beg of you to be, not only men and women of prayer, but intercessors. When Jesus saw Jerusalem He wept over it. God is looking for people who will weep over this city and every city in these islands. What's your answer? You can't leave this meeting the same way as when you came in. You have got to do something. You have got to make a decision.

In closing, I am going to ask everyone of you to close your eyes, bow your heads. I am going to ask you now, "Are you satisfied with your prayer life?" What's your answer? I know what many of you are saying: "No, I am not. I am not the man of prayer I ought to be. But I want to be able to pray. I want to be an intercessor. I've got loved ones who are on their way to hell and I want to pray them to Jesus." You really mean that? If you do, make a commitment of yourself to Him, that He might make you an intercessor.

Chapter 13

Motivation

By Brother Andrew

You know we face a terrific revolution of hatred in the world today. The Communists have joined hands even though they hate each other. And we Christians who say that we love one another, we've never been able to find our brother's hand, much less his heart. But in Love China, God brought us together and He gave us a burden on our hearts for China and for the world.

Mao Tse-tung in his *Selected Works* in the first page of his article entitled "Analysis of the Classes in Chinese Society," posed two questions: "Who are my enemies?" and "Who are my friends?"

Similar questions have been asked by revolutionary leaders throughout history, who had a desire to change the world, and the answer to those two questions determines the action. As Christians we don't have to ask those questions. We have to answer just one question. "Who are we?" Or let me make it even more personal,

"Who am I?" Am I a man who stands under the love of God? Am I a man whose sins are forgiven? Am I a man whose faith is born again by faith in Jesus Christ? Am I a man with a sense of destiny? Am I a man who has been called of Jesus, who said, "Go?" Am I a man who has received the Divine Commission to proclaim the Gospel in the whole world? That is the question you and I have to answer. "Who am I in Christ?"

More than conquerors, through Him who loves us, we have nothing to lose. But who can win the world for Christ? Can you? Can I? And if we find the answer to that certain question, "I can do all things through Christ" then, Christ calls us to change the course of history. But if we want to change the course of history, we had better move into it because if God has done something in Christ Jesus on which the salvation of the whole world depends, and if He has made it known to me, then, I have no choice than to proclaim it and to live it, and to be utterly intolerant of everything that tries to obscure or to ignore, explain, negate, or deny that Great Commission. The open Bible on this platform today, which God so graciously has given to all of us, the very reason for your being here, is because of the liberty in your country to have an open Bible. The ever accusing map of the world forced me into radical action. Is it not my job to win a few souls for Christ? Yes, but the basis of the Great

Commission is to go and make disciples of all nations. And wherever Christ sends me, I must have faith that He will use me to change a nation, that He wants to use me to change China. He wants me to love China and that's more than to just love a Chinese.

I have been so impressed in our conference hall during the last five days. Everytime I looked at that picture behind the platform and saw the hundreds of faces there in that large photograph, I could have cried. There was not one happy face in that picture. Compare those faces, dear conference participants, to the faces of the choir here tonight. Did you see the difference! What made the difference? Jesus Christ made the difference! And when He sends me to China, I must have faith that He's going to change people in their thinking, their lives and their destiny. Because of the preaching of Jesus and the Kingdom of God, I must have faith that this will happen in my generation, or in the next generation through my work.

Now, let us think big of our God. The Church should be on the move today. We should reach every nation. That's why God has now called us for China. And we must get ready and prepare. We must prepare the message and the messenger. We must be motivated for this great task. God has to mobilize us into action. God will give us the Holy Spirit. And with the Holy Spirit, all the power we need to accomplish the great task. God will give us faith. God will give us the open doors so that in this generation China will be reached. But how can the people prepare for war if the trumpet makes an uncertain sound? And how can God prepare His army if you don't make yourself available? Available to the God who bought you with the price of the blood of His Son. Available for whatever He calls you to.

Tonight, we have come. We have to come to a decision. I have prayed that God will make me a crisis man. That wherever I speak, people will have to make a decision. Because it is by decisions that our lives are being changed. Tonight, we have to make a decision. We have to dedicate ourselves to God with all that we are, and all that we will be, and all that we have and all that we will have. It is said that when Oliver Cromwell's Commonwealth found itself very short of silver, so that it couldn't make coins anymore, he sent out men to search for any available silver in Britain or its new colonies. And the men returned and they explained that the statues in the great cathedrals of the world were made of solid silver. It was then that Cromwell issued the famous order, "Let us melt down the saints and put them in circulation." Oh let us allow God to put us into circulation. We don't need saints in the windows. We need saints on the fields. "For thou shalt be my witnesses unto all men." His witnesses to proclaim Christ. Let's not reduce the Great Commission to a mere dialogue, and let not all our knowledge of mission history be the quotations of the saints of the past. They are in heaven today and it is not to their advantage if we keep quoting them. I think we have now quoted enough saints. They have now handed their torch to us. And the question now remains, "Will the next generation, if there is any to be, quote us?" Will they quote us as men and women of God who dared to step out and do the impossible? Will it be written on your tombstone, "He did what he could not!"

You say, "How can I do it?" By faith. And faith is a gift of God. To whom does God give this gift? To those who obey, for those who prove by their obedience that they love Him. I'm also sure that God will test our sincerity, because the Almighty God also works with principles. And in my 20 years of work in the Communist countries, I have discovered this one particular principle. That God will not show us the way to reach the 900 million Chinese in Mainland China if we are not concerned and busy and effective among the 30 million Overseas Chinese. God will not show us the open door into Tibet if we make not every effort to reach the Tibetans that are in Northern India and in Switzerland. We, in Europe, complain that one country totally closed is Albania. There's not a trace of religion left in the country. And even in a prison camp recently, they shot a priest for secretly baptizing a little baby. When will God open the door to Albania? There are as many Albanians in the neighboring country of Yugoslavia as there are in Albania itself. And there are thousands of Albanians in Boston, U.S.A.

We say that the doors to Russia are closed. 250 million Russians are behind barbed wire. But there are millions of Russians outside Russia. And there is only one Russian Bible School in the entire world and that Bible School is in Argentina, South America.

You know what it says in Acts I, verse 8 — "Preach the Gospel in Jerusalem and in Judea and in Samaria and unto the uttermost parts of the world." I have discovered the secret in that verse. It said "and" — it did not say "after." We must reach the 30 million "and" the 900 million. But the 30 million is God's test case. And then, imagine, if we are faithful to the 30 million, God will open the door to the 900 million. Jesus did not say in Jerusalem and then afterwards in Judea, and then afterwards in Samaria and then afterwards in the rest of the world. If the disciples had done this, they would never have come to us. They would have been so discouraged in Jerusalem, they would have given up. They would have said, "We'll never make it. We'll never reach everyone in Jerusalem. There's no sense going to Judea and Samaria." But

Jesus did not say that. He said. "and, and, and." So, we must reach all the Chinese and not say we must first cover it all — the 30 million. And we can go today.

And I can just hear you thinking now. There are enough, of course, who will never go. Because they cannot go. But now, I have given you a nice excuse. Who decided that you cannot go? Oh, your age. Yes. We also work with people of all ages. We work with men and women in our mission. We work with boys and girls. And the oldest girl in our team is only 83. Who said that age is a limitation? Can you show me a verse, a scripture on that? Is 80 years old when you have all of eternity in your possession? Who decides whether or not you're suitable to go? Will you please let God decide it?

I think of a woman like Gladys Aylward No mission wanted her. God said, "Go!" And "go" means a change of location. And that "go" comes to us with so much authority the moment we accept it by faith and obedience, as if coming from Jesus Christ Himself. Then we realize that nothing and no one can stop us. But I tell you this: everyone who can go, and everyone who can give, should make a solid decision today. It's all wrapped up in this long subject of the Lordship of Jesus Christ.

Do you know the secret of the Apostle Paul's success? When he met Jesus Christ for the first time, what was the first question he asked

Jesus? He didn't speak about heaven. He didn't speak about sin, or forgiveness. He didn't ask what he would get out of it. He didn't ask Jesus what he should not do anymore. What was the first thing Paul said to Jesus? "Lord, what do you want me to do?" That was the secret of his success. The Lordship of Christ, he acknowledged straightway. He had met one who was stronger than himself. And immediately, he totally submitted himself to Him. That's the true Christian life. And there is no other Christian life. You know the secret of Judas' failure? I've read through the scriptures on the subject of Judas. It broke my heart to find out the following. Judas never called Jesus, "Lord." Did you know that? Because the moment you say, "Lord," you have got to do what He tells you. Leaving behind your family and your house and your land and your loved ones, to follow the Man of Sorrows, to become part of the suffering Church. The Gospel message is, "Jesus is Lord." And let's proclaim it! We don't proclaim it in the midst of those who are His. The Lordship of Christ should be proclaimed to those that are not His, so that they can bow their knees and confess "Jesus Christ, you are Lord!"

God is working today. Man selects a hero to save him. Oh, you see that strongly in the Communistic system of the world today. But God selects a people to save mankind. His people - that's you and me! The message is more important than the messenger. It's a message that's going to get people in touch with the Almighty God. We are only the messenger. And unless we realize that, then we will not find it difficult anymore to lay down our lives for the brethren because the message is more important than the messenger. God thinks much bigger than we think. And God loves bigger, too. The Bible says, "God loves the nations." That's already recorded in Deuteronomy 33:3. And I believe God loves China as a nation more than any other nation. That's why he made more of them. And now, God calls the people. That's you and I. And if you will pray tonight, "Lord, what do you want me to do?" then God is going to answer. Because we know the solution. It is not to attack China wildly and blindly with a spiritual offensive. It must begin here. But begin it must.

We have heard about the Welsh Revival from our Brother Willis. We heard how churches were opened day and night for over two years. Peoples by the thousands flocked to the churches and got right with God. If that happens in all the countries around China, that sure will hit the headlines of every secret Communist report in Mainland China and in all the newspapers in the world. It will prove that we love God. Now we face today a fanatic, atheistic revolution which actively plans to conquer the whole world with a message that so far is unchallenged. This revolution is being carried out by people with a dedication that is utterly unmatched, and is going ahead with a success that is unprecedented. I ask myself, "Is it because they are unprayed for? Is it because they are unloved?"

Love China '75 will come to a close, but the love for China can never close. Love in action will continue. Love of God, through us. Our prayer has been all through the week, "Oh, Jesus, through us let the people feel your love." It is love in action. It's a love that will motivate us to sacrifice. It will motivate us to go. It will motivate us to give. It will motivate us to live for Christ. It will motivate us to die for Christ. But you can never die for Christ if you don't first live for Him. And when Marx wrote his Communist Manifesto, he wrote those words on the first page, "you have nothing to lose, you have a world to gain."

And that's what I want to tell you today. We have such a tremendous message. God has chosen us. And the Word of God says, "Now, we must please Him who has chosen us." But we must not choose what pleases us. There's only one way out in the chaos of the world today. There's only one way to defend the liberty of your own nation. There's only one way, father and mother, to protect your own family. There's only one way, pastors, to build up your church.

That is to commit all to Jesus Christ. And then, say it and mean it — "Lord, what do you want me to do?" And then, we make more of our lives His responsibility. God will look after us. God will defend us. But how much does God have to take away from us, friends? All through the week I've heard this message. The Church in China is so pure and strong and purged. Can we minister to that suffering Church? We can. If we let God take away from us all that is "not" in Him. And the Church that is truly purged by fire, a Church that can say with the Apostle Paul, "I have been crucified with Christ. Nevertheless, I live. Not that I live, but that Christ lives in me." That Church can never risk anymore. That Church will know no limitations. That Church will know no barriers.

Today, only unbelief is the big limitation. God wants to take it away completely. God wants the spirit of Love China to continue in our hearts. Many of us will take that spirit to our own countries worldwide. And it's going to start fires burning all over the world. It's going to generate prayer all over the world. It is going to raise up intercessions all over the world. Do you want to be a part of it? Then, one day, God will say, "How about answering your own prayer. Go!" Because of your total dedication to Him, because you realize what you are in Christ, you'll find no excuses. Just that intense desire to follow Jesus and to do His Will and to love

China. To love the world. The world as God loves the world and gave Himself for it.

There's a big difference between the revolution of hatred and the revolution of love. As we face this tremendous challenge of the revolution of hatred, we see people kill those who disagree with them. That has taken place all over the Communistic world. We call it persecution and political purges. But in the revolution of love, for which Jesus Christ is mobilizing tonight His troops, where is the revolutionary who has heard His voice and wants to press onwards as a Christian soldier? That revolutionary is ready to lay down his life so that the other fellow will live. And there is no other way.

Love is the way. You are the person. Jesus wants to love China through us. Through you and through me. Do we want to say, "Yes, Jesus?" Do we want to say, "Yes, Lord?" Do we want to say, "Lord, what do you want me to do?" Do you?

I said that I had prayed that God would make me a crisis man. We're living in a time of extreme crisis already. Time is running out on us. God loves the world. He wants to use you. Will you, tonight, make that decision? To be a revolutionary? Simply say, "Yes." God doesn't ask whether you're young or old. He doesn't ask whether you're rich or poor. He doesn't ask whether you're educated or just an ordinary man or woman. God doesn't ask whether you're single or married, but rather, are you rightly related to God through Jesus Christ?

"Do you want to follow Me? To follow whatever I have for you, with all you have and all you are. Will you?" God has spoken in this week to all of us in this seminar. And I can hear China calling. I can hear Russia calling. I can hear the Moslem world calling. And the life of every man and woman and boy and girl of these countries is threatened with destruction. I know the answer. It is Jesus. "Lord, what do you want me to do?" Do you want to say that to Jesus now? If you say, "Yes, I want to," I want you to make it a very simple, basic decision. We have to make decisions as Christians. The very decision to take up your cross daily and follow Him is a tremendous decision. Do we do it consciously each day? If not, that's why we don't grow up in Grace. You must grow up in Him, by making a decision tonight. "Lord, what do you want me to do?"

Let's call on the name of the Lord together, and pray again together the prayer of our conference— "Lord Jesus, through us let the people feel your love." And then we'll pray together, "Lord, what do you want me to do?"

"Lord Jesus, I know that all of heaven is looking on us today. And I know that the forces of hell are watching us now. I know that Satan is trembling now, because there are going to be people here who are going to be real prayer partners. Thank you, Lord, that China is going to feel your love through us. Lord Jesus, through us let the people feel your love. I thank you, Lord, that you're going to answer our prayer because you've said that you hear and answer prayer. And we take you at your word. Also, we want to believe that the ends of the earth will know who Jesus is. Through your love and the power of the Holy Spirit, in Jesus' name we pray. Amen.''

For further literature, prayer letter, and information, write to:

Open Doors
P.O. Box 2020
Orange, California 92669